Rachel Barton studied Theology and Religious Studies at Newnham College, Cambridge, then went on to work in education as a religious education teacher, adviser, consultant, writer, and editor. She lives in northeast England with her family. After the birth of her first baby, she gave up work to spend her time as a stay-at-home mom, to write, and to explore her interests in creativity and spiritual development. She is a Quaker and accompanies others on their faith journeys through retreats, prayer guidance, and spiritual direction.

4 AM Madonnas

**Meditations and Reflections
for Mothers and Mothers-to-Be**

Rachel Barton

Liguori
LIGUORI, MISSOURI

Imprimi Potest:
Thomas D. Picton, C.Ss.R.
Provincial, Denver Province
The Redemptorists

Published by Liguori Publications
Liguori, Missouri
www.liguori.org

Originally published under the same title by the Society for Promoting Christian
Knowledge, London, 2007.

Library of Congress Cataloging-in-Publication Data: 2007930759

ISBN 978-0-7648-1648-2

Liguori Publications, a nonprofit corporation, is an apostolate of the Redemptorists. To
learn more about the Redemptorists, visit Redemptorists.com.

Printed in the United States of America
11 10 09 08 07 6 5 4 3 2 1
First U.S. edition

Contents

Acknowledgments

This book is dedicated to my husband Stephen, to our son Thomas, and to our new baby Luke, whom we were expecting while much of it was being written, with all my love.

It is also for my godchildren: Jacob, Matthew, Rosie, and Joe, and their brothers and sisters.

My thanks go to all the moms who filled in my questionnaire and agreed to be interviewed; I am grateful for your honesty and generosity in sharing your personal experiences, as I am sure readers will be. Thanks also to Stephen for his support, encouragement and constructive comments, and to Thérèse for starting me on this track.

Throughout this book I refer to *Quaker Faith and Practice* (2nd edition). Copies can be obtained from the Quaker Bookshop, Friends House, 173 Euston Road, London NW1 2BJ, England.

I am grateful to the following for permission to print the material listed.

Antonia Rolls, Artist Extraordinaire (<http://www.antoniarolls.co.uk>; <http://www.jesusonthetube.co.uk>) for the cover picture "4 AM Madonna."

David Higham Associates Limited for "The Conceiving" from *The Orchard Upstairs* (1980) by Penelope Shuttle. Used by permission.

Dawna Markova, Ph.D. (<http://www.SmartWired.org>) for "I will not die an unlived life." In *Reclaiming Purpose and Passion*. San Francisco: Conari Press, 2000.

Nicola Slee for "4 AM Madonna" from *The Book of Mary* (London: Society for Promoting Christian Knowledge, 2007).

Society for Promoting Christian Knowledge for "Circle me, Lord" and "O Lord, Creator of all" from *Landscapes of Light: An Illustrated Anthology of Prayers* (2001) by David Adam.

Acknowledgments

The paintbox journaling activity in chapter 1 and the guided visualization based on the Genesis Creation story in chapter 3 first appeared in a different form, and for a different context, in previously published titles for Christian Education: *Creative RE for 14–19 Year Olds* (2006) by Rachel Barker and *Picturing Creation* by Pamela Draycott and Rachel Barker (© Christian Education Publications, 2005).

Introduction

Pregnancy can be a strange process. Having a baby can alter one's life like nothing else. It is a time when friends, relatives, magazines, doctors, and Babies 'R Us all vie for your attention, telling you what you must have, what you need to do, and what you should be feeling. Put five people in a room with a pregnant woman or a new baby and you'll hear five different points of view, if not six! Popular pregnancy and child care manuals can be a confusing medley of helpful information, scary information, wonderful pictures, medical details, lists of things you must eat, things you must not eat, advice to get your baby in a routine, advice to do the opposite, lists of safety measures, dire warnings, superstitions and, at worst, a good deal of scaremongering.

How do we decide what to do? How do we decide which advice is good? In the middle of this outer whirlwind, it is important to find a sense of inner calm. You can transcend the medley and find something spiritual, something of God, in all of this. Many books and magazines shy away from women's inner experiences at this time, afraid perhaps to open Pandora's box. But it is possible to pay positive attention to your feelings, to enjoy exploring your inner experiences, and to discern clearly what is right for you, your baby, and your new family.

This book can help. It is a handbook of reflective exercises and inspiring thoughts for women who wish to explore the spiritual and emotional dimensions of pregnancy and new motherhood. It will help you to ask the questions that don't often get asked. You can dip in and out.

You are beginning a new phase in life—a small new person will depend on you for imaginative support and inspiration, and you need to find that for yourself, too.

Many of the exercises suggested in this book are suitable for use in reflective spiritual life more generally, so while I have related them specifically to pregnancy and motherhood, I hope that you will continue to find them helpful long after you cease to be pregnant and your family grows up.

Theologically, the material I have used and exercises I suggest come from the broad Christian tradition, particularly its contemplative aspects. I have included wisdom from other world faiths and from secular sources, and have tried to be spiritually inclusive. While this book has been written primarily for Christians, it may also appeal to those of all faiths and of none—to anyone interested in exploring the spiritual and emotional side of their experience in such a special phase of life.

RACHEL BARTON

1

What Can Your Baby Show You About God?

—————➤•●•◄=—————

A baby will make love stronger, days shorter, nights longer, bank-roll smaller, home happier, clothes shabbier, the past forgotten, and the future worth living for.

Anon

Pregnancy and babies are all-consuming. Lots of women wonder, "Where am I in all of this?" We can also ask, "Where is God in all of this?" because it's easy to lose sight of God, too. A good place to start is to look at what your baby can show you about God, and when we do that, we might find ourselves as well. As this mother says:

In nothing else is the essence of God more evident than in a child.

Vicki, mother of 4- and 6-year-old daughters

4 AM Madonna

If you are reading this book because you are pregnant, then you are probably getting up several times a night to go to the bathroom. If you are a new mother, you'll be up in the night with your baby. Think of yourself as a 4 AM madonna! Your baby is a child of God—a wonderful, if demanding, gift.

The picture on the front cover of this book is by artist Antonia Rolls. It shows Mary at 4 AM, halo and all, looking exhausted as she jiggles the baby Jesus, in a blue striped sleeper, on her knee. She has bags under her eyes, looks about to cry, and she's brewed a pot of tea to keep her going. The baby is wide awake, perky, and ready to play. Mary's traditional blue gown is decorated with little crosses—the baby Jesus is, at 4 AM, the cross she has to bear. She is the one

1

who is making the self sacrifices—lots of them, all over! Despite her wrung-out face, her halo shines brightly.

We are all used to seeing more traditional pictures of the Madonna and Child—all serene and divine—and especially at Christmas we're used to thinking about what messages the baby Jesus holds. I think this painting is great. It's a very human picture, and very real. When I asked a group of new mothers what they had found most challenging about life with a new baby, one said very frankly, "Coping when wiped out!" This picture shows Mary doing just that. When we have our own babies, we are confronted with the nitty gritty of real life, and also with a miracle. So, let's look at what your baby can show you. Jesus can show us what it's like to be human. Your baby can show you something about what God is like:

> Something of God
> Comes into the world
> With every child that is born.
> There is here with the newborn child
> A divine spark, a light within.[1]
>
> *Rufus M. Jones*

The thoughts that follow are insights about God which were strengthened and developed during my pregnancy—yours may be different. Mine have their roots in my Quaker tradition, but Christians of all denominations will have all sorts of insights. It's important to explore your own, and maybe these ideas can help. Following from the thoughts below I offer some exercises for prayer or reflection as a way of exploring your own experiences. Pregnancy and having a new baby is a time when everything seems to change. By reviewing each day we can start to see God at work.

Maybe you have a faith already. Many of us start with an image of God that has been formed over many years. Sometimes this image comes from our own experience, but often we rely on taught ideas, without realizing it until our lives change and we start to question our assumptions. If this rings true for you, then perhaps you might find it helpful to start to think about well-known words used to describe God, such as father. How does becoming a parent give you new insight into God as a father?

Maybe you don't have a faith background. Having a baby might for the first time bring new and unexpectedly powerful insights and even a changed sense of meaning:

I'm not religious but I think I am quite spiritual. Having Hannah has taught me a much greater sense of empathy with other parents and a genuine belief in the importance of the everyday and the smaller things in life. I now take things slower and enjoy them more. It is an amazing feeling rediscovering things through a child's eyes.

Emma, eight months pregnant and mother
of a 1-year-old daughter

And:

I did not have a faith before I had a baby, now I think I might. It is a profoundly moving thing to have a child and when you look at them, it's hard not to think they were "sent by God" in some sense.

Hannah, mother of an 8-month-old daughter
and a 2½-year-old daughter

See if the ideas below set off your own thoughts, then have a go at the activities that follow—it may not be easy to find some free time, but, who knows, 4 AM might be a good time to reflect!

God as Creator

A tiny baby makes you very aware of God's creation and I found myself marveling at their tiny fingers and toes! It's amazing how each baby is very different and that made me appreciate the uniqueness.

Jane, mother of an 8-year-old daughter
and a 5-year-old son

As Christians, we may have a strong belief in God as Creator, however that may be understood in today's world. It is a poetic image that unfolds for different people in different ways. It conveys something of the power of God and our dependence on him, and relationship with him. Also, it can reveal something special about the nature of created beings. I found thinking about God as Creator was particularly meaningful during my pregnancy, because pregnant women can be seen as sharing in the role of creating.

I came across this idea when I was pregnant:

Creativity is the gift we were given on the eighth day of creation. In naming and re-making the world we are co-workers with God, and whether we are making a garden or a meal, a painting or a piece of furniture or a computer program, we are sharing in an ongoing act of creation through which the world is constantly remade.[2]

To explore this you might like to think of something other than a baby whom you have created or given birth to—it could be anything, from a painting or story to a project at work, a garden, a recipe or a charity event, or an idea or theory developed over time. Anyone who has ever experienced a creative process like this will know how absorbing and stimulating it can be, how one can lose oneself in it, and also how invested one becomes in its success. A fascinating aspect of this process is one that often goes unnoticed— but it is one which I think is reflected in God's creator relationship with us, and in our own creative process of pregnancy and bringing up a child. There is always a point at which the created becomes something more than the sum of the parts of the work of the creator and the raw materials. There is always a point at which something unconscious takes over and the creative spirit starts to produce something completely new and original—the created thing takes on its own momentum and often changes from, or exceeds, the creator's original conception. Created beings are not just products of a creator, they have their own spirit and character—the creative spark within them takes on a life of its own, and the creator must recognize this as the time to let go. We see this reflected in the Genesis Creation story when Adam and Eve use their imaginations to name the animals, and when they start to go their own way down a path that God had not intended but which he allows to unfold.

This is what makes the process of conception, pregnancy, birth, and child-rearing so fascinating: a process started by two people becomes its own new creation—a baby—who may well bear traces of the original creators but will be unique. We are wise when we enjoy the process and enjoy our role in shaping it, without trying to control the outcome or final product—I think this is true for the whole of a growing child's life. Elizabeth Watson writes: "We should respect their right to grow into their own wholeness, not just the wholeness we may wish for them." One of the true wonders I have experienced is watching my baby's innate personality unfold. Thomas looks a little like me and a little like my husband, but he is not a "mini-me," or a "mini-Stephen," he is a miniature new person, an original!

This mother says of her son:

> It's amazing to see him growing and learning and to see his personality and individuality coming out as he develops.
>
> *Jenna, seven months pregnant and*
> *mother of a 2-year-old son*

Allowing the creative process to unfold free from constraint or coercion is one of the joys of being human. It reflects God's relationship with us, and it's an experience profoundly illustrated in parenthood.

Being pregnant and having a child has opened my eyes to another aspect of God's creation: there is room for imperfection and for taking risks. The possibility of having a child with special needs, either at birth or later, is a risk all parents take. I have friends who have suffered miscarriages, and of course we can never know why. It is a risk of pregnancy that still doesn't tend to stop us hoping and bravely yearning to create a new life. Perhaps, when we experience things going wrong and we might feel God is remote or has failed to act, God actually grieves with us for his creation and his loss. As Christians we may think of God as all-powerful, yet to me it is clear from creation that God may be far more about beauty, originality, joy, risk, and drama rather than perfection. I have started to think of God the creator as an impressionist painter rather than an architect. Painters use a broad brush, not a fine pencil, and the strokes are not always precise or measured. They don't mark their canvas out in neat, exact squares; they use a rough sketch that might be erased and drawn over several times. Yet the outcome can be breathtaking. Imperfections and glitches are absorbed to become part of a beautiful whole. Volcanoes, avalanches, quirks of nature, diversity of experience, and human variety are not discarded at the drawing board because they add something of value—a certain unpredictability, an unexpected twist, which challenge us to notice the painting, to respect it, and not look at it with complacency. My husband has his own version of this way of thinking: he sees God as a storyteller who does not have the end of the story decided or written down in a carefully designed structure but who allows the characters to unfold and surprise him. God may have made a covenant with us for an ultimately joyful ending, and certainly the characters have many things chosen for them, but otherwise they are free and the story unfolds as it is being told.

When you think of your role in creation, do you see yourself as a character in a book, a brush stroke of color on a canvas, or a carefully designed structure? How do you see your baby? What might your insights tell you about God?

The Fertile, Feminine Side of God

I have grown closer to my own mother and understand how much she loves me now.

Tess, mother of a 6-month-old daughter

Pregnancy and birth are unique and bonding female experiences. Many women find that their sense of their fertility helps them to understand the feminine side of God. Your body is working with God to create new life. What is happening inside you can be compared to what happened in the universe at the point of creation.

Sometimes contemporary life suggests pregnancy is a time of ugliness or unattractiveness—nothing could be further from the truth. Why not take some time each day to honor your new pregnant shape? It's easy to feel fat and frumpy and sick, so it can be a great boost to celebrate the miracle happening on the inside by paying some special attention to the outside. Choose something that you like about your physical appearance while you are pregnant.

Enhance it and pay special attention to it each day. I felt exhausted much of the time, but my hair and nails were better than ever, so I made time to wash and style my hair and treated myself to manicures. I felt proud of my bump—we took photos of it growing bigger and bought some fragrant massage creams. If you find it difficult to find something you like, ask friends what sorts of things they do to help them feel good about their body. This is more than just superficial pampering—pregnancy is a physical experience and has a physical manifestation that can be revered and valued.

Also, surround yourself with positive images of pregnancy. The artist Gustav Klimt celebrated the female form in his art and the pregnant women in his portraits have an allure and sensuality that capture a real sense of beauty. The symbols in these paintings show that he considered pregnancy to be a fertile and creative state that transcends the destructive and malign influences in human experience, such as death and poverty. He described one woman, in a picture called *Hope I* (1903), as "a living vessel in which the hope of mankind is ripening." The colors are vibrant and the women have confident, serene expressions on their faces in this painting and in *Hope II*—both pictures can be found in an Internet search. So can other images if you type in a search term such as "maternity" or "motherhood"—see if you can find some that appeal to you. They are a good antidote to the less glamorous aspects of pregnancy that we all experience!

There are celebrations of fertility, pregnancy, and women's creating role in literature too. Poet Penelope Shuttle writes:

The Conceiving

Now

> you are in the ark of my blood
> in the river of my bones
> in the woodland of my muscles
> in the ligaments of my hair
> in the wit of my hands
> in the smear of my shadow
> in the armada of my brain
> under the stars of my skull

in the arms of my womb
Now you are here
you worker in the gold of flesh

I am not sure whether she is writing from the perspective of the mother, describing the baby inside her, or maybe the role of her partner in helping to create the child, or if she is writing from the perspective of the baby as it knits itself together from her own cells. What do you think? Either way, the poem for me is a powerful description of the infinite wonder of this creative, fertile, and feminine process.

Welcome to the World by Nikki Siegen-Smith[3] provides a lovely collection of poems and photographs celebrating pregnancy, birth, and parenthood from cultures across the world. Why not keep your own collection of inspiring quotes and beautiful images that you come across while you are pregnant and build your own anthology in a scrapbook?

God's Nurturing and Indulgent, Unconditional Love

I just look in wonder at my boy every day and think how lucky we are to have you...the most wonderful thing about becoming a mother is the amazing connection between Thomas and me.
Harriet, mother of a 10-month-old son

We are both chosen and choosing when we bring babies into the world. We are fortunate and responsible. We are also loved and we are doing something important—we need to take extra special care of ourselves.

I have read somewhere that a pregnant woman lolling about on the sofa uses the same amount of energy as a nonpregnant woman hiking up a hill. Growing a baby is hard work. Do we need a better reason for nurturing ourselves? In our busy prepregnancy lives, however, our idea of nurturing ourselves might be a glass of wine with dinner or a speedy bath at the end of the day. Indulgence may have negative connotations of weakness—extra pudding, or being overemotional. We may feel we put more into nurturing others than into nurturing ourselves, such as when we remember relatives' birthdays, phone a friend in need, listen sympathetically to our partner's day, or go the extra mile for a colleague. But nurturing takes on a whole new importance during pregnancy and as we start life with a baby. In spiritual terms the nurturing or indulgent love God has for each of us is positive and extravagant, and that's the kind we need to be thinking about.

The strong feelings of love and support that can be prompted by a pregnancy can begin to give us more insight into the indulgent love of God. These feelings of love and protection may be felt toward the unborn baby, and may be felt by a partner toward a pregnant woman. They are reflected in the smiles and solicitude pregnant women receive when they are out and about. Pregnancy manuals often encourage women to show a bit more of them toward themselves at this time.

For many these feelings of being blessed are echoes of God's feelings of love and support toward all of us. As this Muslim mother says:

Now that I know how much, how deeply, a mother loves her baby, I can at least slightly imagine how much God loves all people as in Islam God has said that he loves everyone even seventy times more than a mother loves her baby. So it has strengthened my faith and it's far more easy for me to leave every worry of my life to God.

Robina, mother of a 7-month-old son

I related very well to the following words when I came across them in another source:[4]

Our lives have recently been transformed by the birth of a baby daughter. Nothing we read or were told could prepare us for the total revolution in our lives which the arrival of this beautiful spirit into our midst has brought…That moment of timelessness and joy was like a glimpse of heaven, seen through the miracle of birth…with the endless possibilities for discovery, growth, and love for all three of us.

What took me completely by surprise was how all-consuming new motherhood was—especially on days when my baby had colic, or early teething pains, and seemed to cry all day. No one really prepares new mothers for that. It can be relentless and exhausting at times, and even on better days when you are loving the experience, there is very little room at first for anything else. I felt that all I could do—and what I was actually being asked to do—was to pour myself into this little person, to give myself over completely to looking after him, and with joy, not begrudgingly. I found this outpouring very demanding, but we had planned and wanted this baby and I knew this period would not last forever, which meant I could do it without resentment.

In Christian theology, there is a term for this sort of self-emptying. *Kenosis* refers to the self-emptying of God to become the human person of Jesus at the Incarnation. It is the means by which Jesus is fully human, and it is a process motivated by God's love for us. God freely gives up something of himself in order to be human, with all the feelings and experiences and limitations that brings, so that love can have a profound effect in the world. I think this means that God can relate very well to what mothers do! I like it when abstract theological ideas (however they are understood) find a practical expression in the lives and experience of ordinary people, and I find this link between love and self-emptying very apt, because for me the demands of new motherhood were made easier by the intense feelings of love which I felt when first handed my baby and which I found grew immeasurably as time went on (something else no one can prepare you for!), so I kept hold of the wonder and joy of such a revolution in my life as I gave myself over to nurturing my baby. I know that it's easy to lose this perspective, though—especially at 4 AM—and I know that many women use less positive words to describe it: "claustrophobic," "nothing of myself left."

Becoming a parent is a maturing process. Probably for the first time in our lives, we are asked to put our own needs second in favor of a tiny, dependent person whose survival and well-being rely on our willingness and ability to meet his or her needs first. This requires us to be big, generous people. It requires us to love and to give abundantly, regardless of how we feel. It doesn't require us to be sour-faced martyrs and of course it is right that we look after ourselves well, but we do have new and important responsibilities. We need to be mindful of the effect on our children of our tone of voice, the labels we use, and how welcoming our arms are. A 4 AM madonna has a choice when faced with a screaming newborn, a toddler in a tantrum, unspeakable diapers, mastitis and, chronic exhaustion. A 4 AM madonna can go to her child tenderly and with compassion, freely showing her unconditional love, or she can blame the baby for being difficult and for making her life miserable. She can choose to be irritable and sarcastic, or gentle and nurturing. It is the generosity of unconditional love shown in abundance that helps children to grow up with a deep-rooted sense of their own well-being and of the safety of the world in which they live. Where it is not shown or where it is held back in reserve, children can grow up feeling that there is something "not OK" about themselves and the world. What power we have! It is a power shared by God, who chooses to show us unconditional love so that we can feel whole. Your baby's first experience of God's love will be through your love and through the way you choose to respond to his or her needs. This may come easily, or it may be harder, particularly if your baby has a different temperament to you or your partner. Elaine Aron's book *The Highly Sensitive Child*[5] has good ideas for recognizing and honoring all sorts of different temperaments within a family—it does require time, effort, and a willingness to love generously. But ultimately, showing our love unreservedly and welcoming others for who they are is more satisfying and rewarding than not, because our relationships are more likely to flourish happily and be a source of joy in our lives.

As Christians, we hopefully find it encouraging rather than daunting to know that the sort of selfless outpouring of love, generosity, and commitment we are being asked to give is the sort that God gives unconditionally to us. Maybe God finds it just as difficult sometimes, when we behave as if we are unwanted, unloved, unaccepted, or when we make demands on those who do love us just because we feel selfish and difficult. But God's indulgent love never wavers and it's always given in abundance because we are his children. However, it needs to be acknowledged that sadly this may be a different sort of love to the one some people grow up imagining coming from God. Christians compare God's love to that of a father, yet for many the thought of God's love may have sterner undertones. God is also thought of as a judge, and a king, and even the image of a father is helpful only insofar as relationships with our own fathers are healthy and whole. Many people find their image of God is bound up with their childhood experience of their own parents. For some this love may have been more critical or conditional and less supportive than the image of God as father is meant to convey. If this rings true for you, it may help to reexamine your image of God and to reflect on where in your life you have experienced love that is life-enhancing. For others, happily, having a baby might lead to a greater understanding of how much their own parents really did put into nurturing and loving them, and consequently into what God's love for us means, providing an inspiring model.

Many women have mixed feelings, or ambivalent feelings, about their pregnancies. Many babies are surprises—some are shocks. In the end, it is probably best to be honest with yourself now about your feelings. Acknowledge them, accept them, and validate them—then use them to help you to plan for a happy family life. Conversations with trusted friends, relatives, or support groups can help many people to discover and accept their feelings. In the gospels, the news of Mary's baby comes as a shock—it is news she questions before accepting. It is not an ideal or a fully supported pregnancy. She takes time out to visit her cousin Elizabeth as she comes to terms with the direction her life has taken (see Luke 1:39–40). If this is how you feel, then you might find some of the later sections of this book helpful. An unwanted gift is still a gift generously given and specially chosen, and can still inspire a positive response. Our journey through life can take unexpected turns—we may find ourselves in hard or unexpected places, but in the end these can also be times of great blessing, joy, and renewal. So it's important to ask, what is your true experience, and how, after accepting how you feel, might you use it positively? How will your experience be a life-enhancing one, for you and your baby?

In the New Testament the Holy Spirit is sent to be an advocate —the divine Spirit is on our side, speaks for us, supports us, and defends us, especially when we're faced with adversity. I find this a really helpful and encouraging image. Perhaps pregnancy, with its accompanying enhanced feelings of love and hope for a new life, and good intentions for our own role as a parent, can be the ideal time for coming to a deeper understanding of God. Let's try tuning into our true rather than our taught experiences of him! This can help us to recognize and accept the special gifts and blessings our life brings, and the responsibilities those request. It can be a time when we might really begin to understand how much God loves us:

> The overwhelming love you feel for a baby shows something of God's love for us. Creating a new life is an amazing thing, also the love you feel for your child…motherhood is very rewarding. Life is precious and children are a gift.
>
> *Rachel, 16 weeks pregnant and mother of five sons,*
> *aged between 1 and 8*

God's Presence in Everyday Life

> Don't forget to enjoy every moment.
> *Louise, mother of a 1-year-old daughter and a 3-year-old son*

How can you increase your awareness and become more mindful of each special moment, and of what the Spirit might be saying to you in those moments? Do you allow space periodically for this to happen—listening time?

When you pray or reflect, or simply make yourself available for a few minutes with the words "OK, here I am," try to notice if any words come to you from the Spirit. I don't mean hearing voices, just noticing words that you may find yourself thinking or convictions that suddenly seem clear. This may not happen every time, and it may happen when you least expect it.

On the way to my twelve-week ultrasound scan, I was worried about finding something wrong with the baby. Every story of disappointment or distress I had ever heard came flooding back as I tried to expect the best but also prepare for the worst. I wanted to feel excited about the prospect of seeing our baby dancing around on the screen, but instead I just felt trepidation, as if about to face a time of testing. After some time I prayed a "just letting you know that this is how I'm feeling" sort of prayer, sending my feelings wordlessly out there, and suddenly felt a much greater sense of calm. The words,

"Trust—this baby is meant for you" came to me very clearly, and stayed with me until we went in for the scan.

For me, this was a reassuring experience—there was no guarantee of perfection or a problem-free scan, but it did help me to feel whatever happened was meant to be. In the end the scan was fine—a delightful experience—but sometimes we have to trust in a state of not knowing. We have to stand beside our own feelings of confusion or emptiness, and simply trust if we cannot immediately discern a clear way. Pregnancy can be an experience that inspires trust and reliance—in God and in other people, as life at this time can't always be ordered, predicted, or controlled in the way we might be used to. We need to get used to waiting to see, and in the course of this we can become much more aware of the presence of God and of the loving concern of other people in our daily lives.

Other words that came to me during times of prayer or reflection during my pregnancy were "rest," "receive," and "enjoy." Each came at just the right time, usually when I was doing quite the opposite of what I needed. This showed me a lot about God's continual presence and indulgent love, as well as about the need to trust and to relinquish control.

Try looking for that of God, or the Light, in each day, encounter, and experience—either as you go or as you look back during a period of quiet at the end of the day. Notice what is lifegiving and energizing, and what drains you. Gravitate toward, and give thanks for, the former. Notice moments to enjoy. What do these experiences show you about God and his desires for you?

This mother gives good advice:

> Try to enjoy every stage of your growing baby. Overlook any hardship you face, as it will all pass very quickly and you'll just be left with memories, so make beautiful memories out of it.
>
> *Robina, mother of a 7-month-old son*

I think these are wise words.

The activities that follow are designed to help you to engage with the process of recognizing God's presence in everyday life more easily. The point of recognizing God's presence in key moments is that you can then appreciate them and give thanks for them, which will make your day better and also deepen your relationship with God. They will help to form your beautiful memories.

These activities are art-based, because sometimes it can be hard to find the right words and abstract images can help, but you don't need to be able to draw—just give them a try!

Paintbox Prayers: Using Color and Shape as Symbols

Color and shape are used in religions as symbols to express the abstract or transcendent—feelings, beliefs, and experiences which cannot be easily described. And when you're a 4 AM madonna, there are plenty of those around! Exploring shape and color in prayer can help us to understand this form of expression, and also deepen our own reflective capacity.

I like the work of Sister Sheila Julian Merryweather, CSC. In her book *Colourful Prayer*,[6] she uses this poem to show how colors can symbolize feelings, characteristics, and concepts[7]:

The Paintbox

I had a paintbox—
Each colour glowing with delight,
I had no red for wounds or blood,
I had no black for an orphaned child,
I had no white for the face of the dead,
I had no yellow for burning sands.
I had orange for joy and life,
I had green for buds and blooms,
I had blue for clear blue skies,
I had pink for dreams and rest,
So I sat down and painted
Peace.

If you like art, look at a selection of famous paintings that use color to convey emotion or character: try *Black on Grey* (1969) by Mark Rothko, which is a large canvas of the colors in the title. How might you feel if you looked at this for a long time? Depressed? Drained? Bleak? Then switch to *Yellow Painting* by Barnett Newman. How might you feel with this on your wall? Cheerful? Energized? Or even more depressed? *Green Stripe (Madame Matisse)* is an effective painting, too. Matisse has painted this portrait of his wife with a green stripe dividing her face into two halves. He uses the different colors to show two different sides of her personality: cool and warm. These paintings can all be found through Internet image searches.

What Do Different Colors Represent for You?

Color has different associations for different people. Take some colored pencils, paints, or crayons and make your own diagram like the example on page 17. Color each circle with a different color, then match them with the different emotions—draw lines to make links that feel right to you between the colors and the feelings: you can add more, and choices are personal and may be different for everyone. Having a baby is a time when feelings run high—do this activity according to what you feel now, rather than what you feel usually.

Which colors do you associate with different emotions?

What Do Different Shapes Represent for You?

Now pick two or three of your color/feeling combinations. Draw a quick shape—without thinking too much or wondering what it will look like to others—using that color to represent that emotion. There are some examples from my own journal on page 18, from a time when I was experimenting with using color and shape in my prayer life, inspired by *Colourful Prayer*.

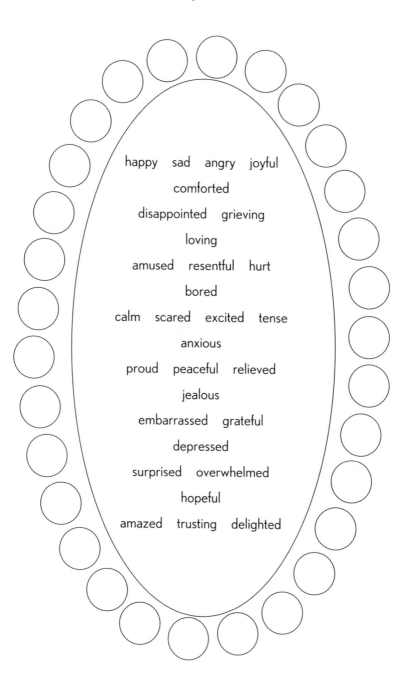

happy   sad   angry   joyful
comforted
disappointed   grieving
loving
amused   resentful   hurt
bored
calm   scared   excited   tense
anxious
proud   peaceful   relieved
jealous
embarrassed   grateful
depressed
surprised   overwhelmed
hopeful
amazed   trusting   delighted

Positive feelings such as happiness, excitement, peace.

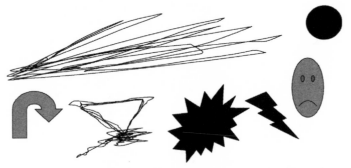

And more negative feelings like anger, disappointment, boredom.

Paintbox Prayers and Journals

Think about the traditional role of a written journal—people write to record and reflect on events and experiences in their lives. Maybe you already do this. Some famous examples, both real and fictional, spring to mind: Anne Frank, Bridget Jones, Virginia Woolf, Adrian Mole, Anais Nin. A paintbox journal is similar but uses the sort of coloring and doodling you have just tried, instead of words.

Take a few moments of quiet one evening to think back over your day. Starting in the morning, think through each moment and jot down the different feelings you had as the day went on. Many of these feelings may be related to your pregnancy or baby. The Examen prayer in the box below might be a helpful method—this style of prayer was developed by Saint Ignatius and Christians have used it for centuries to reflect on their day.

> *Follow Saint Ignatius' teaching*
> *and take a few minutes of quiet each evening*
> *to think back over your day:*
>
> For what moment am I most grateful?
> For what moment am I least grateful?
>
> *There are lots of different ways to ask these questions.*
> *Pick a formula that works for you:*
>
> When was I happy? When was I sad?
>
> When did I give and receive the most love?
> When did I give and receive the least love?
>
> When did I feel the most creative?
> When did I feel the most destructive?
>
> What made me feel most alive?
> What made me feel most tired?
>
> What was the high point?
> What was the low point?
>
> *What made me feel colorful?*
> *What made me feel gray?*

For instance, one day of my own during my thirty-first week of pregnancy looked like this:

AM Difficult morning: my obstetrician thinks the baby isn't growing properly and sent me for an ultrasound scan: *depressed and scared.*

Lunch time After a long wait, had the scan. Everything is fine —one healthy baby! *happy.*

PM Arrived home to find my little dog very ill: *anxious.* An old friend phoned for a chat: *surprised.*

Evening My husband cooked dinner and washed up: *loving.*

Then match your feelings with the colors you chose earlier. Mine were:

AM Difficult morning—my obstetrician thinks the baby isn't growing properly and sent me for an ultrasound scan: *depressed (gray) and scared (black).*

Lunch time After a long wait, had the scan. Everything is fine —one healthy baby! *happy (pink).*

PM Arrived home to find my little dog very ill: *anxious (orange).* An old friend phoned for a chat: *surprised (white).*

Evening My husband cooked dinner and washed up: *loving (red).*

Try drawing your day using the colors and shapes you thought about earlier. Remember that no one else knows what your colors and shapes represent—they can be abstract doodles or more concrete designs. This can be an anonymous exercise, but a greatly expressive one. You can see a black-and-white copy of mine on page 21.

You might like to look at your finished paintbox journal and pray a paintbox prayer. Ask God to help you to review, reconcile, and resolve the different feelings and actions it records. What made you feel colorful and what made you feel gray? Some Christians find it helpful to imagine Jesus sitting next to them as a friend as they do this. Ask the Spirit to help you to notice the things you regret and the things you found nurturing. Try to do this in a spirit of enlightenment: are the things that felt good motivated by love, joy, compassion, and peace, or by status, materialism, and fear? When our desires are rooted in the Spirit we feel content, and that is where God can be found. Allow yourself to feel sorrow for what might have been better; try not to be self-judging but ask for guidance. Allow yourself to feel gratitude for what went well, and give thanks.

What does this review reveal to you about what God is like, and where God may be present in your day? Is this different from traditional views or your own, maybe long-held, assumptions? Are there any surprises? Use this special time in your life to get to know God more deeply, however you experience him, and be prepared for some pleasant surprises.

You could make a quick note of this review next to your picture.

Why not keep a paintbox journal and pray a paintbox prayer for each day, week, or month in your pregnancy? This would be a creative and insightful way of staying in touch with your ever-changing feelings at this time, and would also be a very personal and unusual way of recording an extraordinary period of your life. Once my baby was born, I found it encouraged me to look for flashes of color in gray days, and to enjoy nighttime feedings as colorful times.

Many people find this way of recording their feelings and actions helps them to discern God's desires for them over a period of time. It helps them to notice and to stay in touch with their own desires, values, and happiness. It can bring them to a deeper and more real relationship with God.

These ideas can be used and adapted in other aspects of your spiritual life, particularly if you keep a regular journal:

- To explore and express your inner thoughts and feelings
- To record personal responses to encounters and experiences
- To convey feelings that cannot easily be expressed (e.g., a life-changing experience, a spiritual moment, hope, wonder, trepidation, ambivalence, a response to prayer or to a guided visualization)
- To convey difficult concepts such as loss/death/bereavement; reincarnation/the afterlife; "then/now" or "perfect world/real world" contrasts; anger; justice; peace; love; awe and creation
- To serve as a starting point for trying to empathize with the feelings of others

- To develop the reflective skills of thinking symbolically and expressing yourself in abstract terms when words are not enough
- To deepen your understanding of religious symbolism, decorative art in churches, and nonverbal aspects of worship including some forms of prayer and meditation.

Babies are necessary to grown ups. A new baby is like the beginning of all things—wonder, hope, a dream of possibilities.

Eda J. LeShan, author and educator

2

Prayer and Responding to Feelings, Thoughts, and Memories

A baby is God's opinion that life should go on.
Carl Sandburg, historian, novelist, and poet (1878–1967)

A baby can turn your emotional life upside down! Here we'll look at why that might sometimes be the case, and at different ways of regaining a sense of inner calm so that we too can feel like the psalmist who wrote:

> I have calmed and quieted my soul, like a child quieted at its mother's breast; like a child that is quieted is my soul. *(RSV)*
> *Psalm 131:2*

We'll also look at some different ways of praying, because regular prayer and reflection will help you to retain your self-confidence and inner peace and to be more aware of God's supporting presence as you deal with the myriad of feelings, thoughts, and memories that pregnancy and new motherhood can throw at you.

While we can reflect here on the normal emotional ups and downs a range of pregnant women and new moms may experience, it is beyond the scope of this book to address severe postnatal depression (PND). However, if you are suffering, I would urge you to see your physician for an assessment and to pursue all options as you try to cope with this debilitating and all-too-common condition. Health professionals will have access to well-researched ways of measuring PND and will be able then to recommend the most appropriate treatment for you. It could be that a combination of therapy, medication, spiritual direction, and nutritional treatment could all help. Some of the reflective exercises in this book could help you to discern your feelings and needs more clearly, but do talk to your physician or visiting nurse as well.

23

Childhood Memories

Memories from one's own childhood, often triggered during pregnancy, may be happy and inspiring, but some may also feel darker and more disturbing. Either way, memories of our own early life contribute to our emotional feelings when we have a new baby.

If your memories are difficult for you, then this may be a helpful thought: all these memories need to be acknowledged and owned, and some may need to be dealt with openly and with other people, but some may be better dealt with internally. They can still be validated. Some garden images might be helpful—flowers are beautiful, but have their roots in dark, messy soil. Are there beautiful things that can grow and flourish out of your own dark and messy experiences? My spiritual director suggested imagining a bulb growing in the dark. You know it is there—you have planted it, so it is not forgotten, but no one else can see it. What they do see is what it yields—the plant that grows from it. Tap the creative potential of darker thoughts and memories by looking for the beauty they might yield—this might, for instance, be an internal decision to bring up your own child differently, or to provide something you feel you missed out on, or simply a resolution to be attentive to your child's needs, feelings, and concerns and to ensure as much as you can that the other people they have contact with are respectful of them, too.

Another helpful thing might be to imagine a conversation between yourself as you are now and yourself as a child. What would you like to say to the little girl or teenager you once were? What would she say to you? Either close your eyes and imagine the conversation, or try writing it down—either in two columns, one for you now and the other for your younger self, or in the style of a script for a play. This is designed to be a healing exercise, so be gentle with each other, and befriend each other. You may find it helpful to imagine yourselves sitting together in God's light as you talk.

Of course, many of us have childhood memories of people and experiences that were positive, loving, and nurturing and have helped to shape the sort of person we are today. Identifying some of these might also be insightful—partly for your own self-knowledge and partly to help you to think about how you would like to bring up your own child. Staying with the garden imagery, imagine a tree growing tall and strong—could this be you? Your roots run deep and secure and support you now as an adult. Can you identify any of these roots? For example, perhaps you enjoyed a close relationship with a friend, sibling, parent, or grandparent. Maybe a particular teacher, author, or public figure was a strong influence for you. Experiences as well as people may have been formative—a trip somewhere special or a life-changing event, even the place you lived, and maybe you enjoyed much-loved pets.

Try sketching a tree shape, with roots below the ground and branches above. Along the roots record your positive influences. In the branches, write down the qualities and characteristics that these experiences or people helped you to develop and that help to make you the person you are today.

Notice how key elements of your childhood have helped you to blossom—remember that this can be true of both happy memories and darker memories. What might this tell you about your wishes for your own baby? Add to your sketch fruit that will drop from the tree and nurture the soil to help new trees to grow—these are the fruits of your own experiences and character. Think about the qualities that you have that you can use to help nurture your baby, and write these inside the fruit in your sketch.

As you do this, you might like to reflect on the words of this poem by Dawna Markova:

I Will Not Die an Unlived Life[1]

I will not die an unlived life.
I will not live in fear
of falling or catching fire.
I choose to inhabit my days,
to allow my living to open me,
to make me less afraid
more accessible,
to loosen my heart
until it becomes a wing,
a torch, a promise.
I choose to risk my significance,

to live so that which came to me as seed
goes to the next as blossom,
and that which came to me as blossom,
goes on as fruit.

And on the sentiments of this mother:

Life is a really, really wonderful gift!

Tracey, mother of an 8-month-old daughter

World Events

After having my baby I really didn't want to watch TV programs that highlighted the downside of human nature. I wanted to enjoy my baby. I loved him with an intensity I could never have imagined, and the thought of him being harmed or tainted by the less than wholesome—or downright violent—aspects of our world felt awful. So did the thought of any tragic accident befalling Stephen or me. Part of my creating a home environment conducive to loving and bringing up a whole new person, for me meant turning off the TV and the news at first. I couldn't let it in for a while because it jarred with my idea of what I wanted my brand-new baby to experience in the world into which he was born. This may sound unrealistic—certainly unsustainable—but the sentiments behind it were, and are, very real indeed. All this leads me to ask, if we have an idea of the kind of world we would like for our new babies, what might we be able to do at home, in our local communities, and in the world to bring it one step nearer? And how might we help our children to live in the world they have inherited without being influenced by it in a destructive way? How will we equip them to live in the light?

Many pregnant women feel a curious detachment from, and/or distress about, world events, even before they hold their newborns. I found it difficult to watch the news or to read papers then too, because I alternated between feeling very tearful about the important things happening in my baby's new world, and very distracted by the more important things happening inside me. Some of the detachment and even irritation could be explained by the fact that limited time and energy makes you more likely to want to focus only on what matters the most to you. But the distress and indignation may point to something else—both to a new emotional vulnerability felt by many people once they become parents, and to a deeper sense of the cosmic importance of your new child. I remember a feeling of irrational indignation and also a certainty that everything must be all right for this baby—that society has a responsibility to honor its little miracles by making sure all will be well in the world.

Mary's Magnificat in Luke's Gospel reflects such feelings that all must be well in the world in the light of the momentous event of a new baby. A close reading of the Magnificat shows Mary to be a deeply spiritual person, aware of both God's power and grace and of her own feelings. She is not unquestioning—not immediately accepting or joyful of the news of her pregnancy—yet she is both prayerful and discerning in her awareness of the importance of what she is caught up in. She is also radical in her social concern for the poor, for the political concerns of her day. Her song is very similar to Hannah's song in the Hebrew Scriptures. Hannah was the mother of Samuel and was thought to be unable to have children. She prays for many years before becoming pregnant. Both Mary and Hannah sing songs of praise to God about their new pregnancies. They sing songs that reflect the strong and sometimes contradictory feelings about both the miracle and the world which many pregnant women feel.

Placed side by side, the similarities between Mary's Magnificat and Hannah's song (pages 28 and 29) are clear. You might like to take two different colored pens and find these passages in your own Bible or download the text (try <http://www.oremus.org>)—underline the similar themes with one color, and with the other underline any words or phrases that reflect your own feelings about your pregnancy.

Mary's Magnificat
Luke 1:46–55 (NIV)

And Mary said:
"My soul glorifies the LORD
and my spirit rejoices in God my Savior,
for he has been mindful
of the humble state of his servant.
From now on all generations will call me blessed,
for the Mighty One has done great things for me—
holy is his name.
His mercy extends to those who fear him,
from generation to generation.
He has performed mighty deeds with his arm;
he has scattered those who are proud
in their inmost thoughts.
He has brought down rulers from their thrones
but has lifted up the humble.
He has filled the hungry with good things
but has sent the rich away empty.
He has helped his servant Israel,
remembering to be merciful
to Abraham and his descendants for ever,
even as he said to our fathers."

Hannah's Song
1 Samuel 2:1–10 (NIV)

Then Hannah prayed and said:
"My heart rejoices in the LORD;
in the LORD my horn is lifted high.
My mouth boasts over my enemies,
for I delight in your deliverance.
There is no one holy like the LORD;
there is no one besides you;
there is no Rock like our God.
Do not keep talking so proudly
or let your mouth speak such arrogance,
for the LORD is a God who knows,
and by him deeds are weighed.
The bows of the warriors are broken,
but those who stumbled are armed with strength.
Those who were full hire themselves out for food,
but those who were hungry hunger no more.
She who was barren has borne seven children,
but she who has had many sons pines away.
The LORD brings death and makes alive;
he brings down to the grave and raises up.
The LORD sends poverty and wealth;
he humbles and he exalts.
He raises the poor from the dust
and lifts the needy from the ash heap;
he seats them with princes
and has them inherit a throne of honour.
For the foundations of the earth are the LORD's;
upon them he has set the world.
He will guard the feet of his saints,
but the wicked will be silenced in darkness.
It is not by strength that one prevails;
those who oppose the LORD will be shattered.
He will thunder against them from heaven;
the LORD will judge the ends of the earth.
He will give strength to his king
and exalt the horn of his anointed."

The world we live in doesn't always make it easy for some mothers. Most parenting books are written for people in their twenties and thirties who tend to be in stable relationships, with healthy and wanted babies. The media tends to castigate single mothers and bemoan the teenage pregnancy rate, without always holding absent fathers accountable for their responsibilities. It can be humbling for those of us in happy and committed relationships to remember that God chose an unmarried teenage girl to mother his Son. I hope that women who are in challenging situations can look at Mary and feel encouraged and inspired. She was lucky—an angel was at hand to persuade her partner Joseph to stay with her and support her, but until that point he had other plans (see Matthew 1:18–26). Whatever our personal beliefs about the doctrine of the virgin birth might be, and to be fair to Joseph, we can be certain that he and Mary had not slept with each other. If they had, that would have been a reason for Joseph to bring the wedding date forward, but instead he considers breaking off their relationship. He is sensitive enough to want to do this quietly—otherwise Mary could have been stoned to death for being unfaithful. But even so, as a single mother in her society, she would have faced a life of poverty and disgrace, while bringing up a very special baby. She is in the same position as all those single mothers and pregnant teenagers today who raise their special babies in difficult circumstances, and we might all remember the angel Gabriel's words to her, "Greetings, favored one! The Lord is with you...you have found favor with God" (Luke 1:28, 30).

Poet Nicola Slee has been inspired by Antonia Rolls' picture (on the front cover of this book) to write her own Mary's song. I think it's a great example of a modern-day Magnificat, because in it Mary acknowledges her feelings, reflects on God's purposes, and has a sense of wonder if a very honest fatigue!

4 a.m. Madonna (after Antonia Rolls)

Grim faced, she is desperate for some shut-eye.
Her hands hold the wide awake baby with care,
but she can barely keep her eyes open,
and her mouth slouches with fatigue.
The pot of tea on the sideboard is getting cold.

The line of baby clothes dries slowly.
She wonders why the angel didn't mention
4 a.m. feeds, the grizzling infant,
the vast amounts of washing.
She wonders if God got this tired creating the world,
   and keeping it going.
Placing Jesus back in his cot
and turning to switch out the light,
she thinks she must remember to ask.

There is a strong biblical tradition of women singing to God. Can you write your own Magnificat or song to express your feelings, reactions and hopes at this time?

Overwhelming Feelings About Your Baby

What do you make of this Hindu story?

The child Krishna and his brother Balarama often played in the forest with their friends. Sometimes, their playing would turn to squabbles and they would run to their mother Yasoda. Each would try to get the other into trouble.

One day they came running back from the forest, telling tales.

"Mother!" shouted Balarama. "Krishna has been eating dirt from the ground!"

"Krishna!" said Yasoda. "Is this true?"

"No!" replied Krishna. "It's a lie!"

"Come here and open your mouth!" said his mother. "Let me see!"

So Krishna stood in the sunshine and opened his mouth as wide as he could. Yasoda looked inside and this is what she saw.

She saw the earth and the sky, and everything that had ever been or ever will be. She saw the sun and the moon and the stars and the planets—the whole universe. She saw earth, water, fire, and air. She saw the ocean and the whole of India, the forest, and their village. Then she saw herself, with her son Krishna on her knee, and she was feeding him. She felt as

31

though her head was spinning, and she was overcome with awe and fear. So Krishna closed his mouth so that she would not see any more. And just as she had seen when she looked in his mouth, he sat on her knee and she fed him. Yasoda hugged him, for she knew that he was her son, whom she loved.

But Hindus believe that he was also God. And when people see God too closely, they can become frightened and filled with awe. So Krishna becomes for everyone a little child, a friend and a brother, so that they can love him without being frightened.

Hindus believe that Krishna was one of the incarnations, or *avatars,* of the God Vishnu. God is all-pervading, yet personal. I think this story has some interesting parallels with the New Testament story of the boy Jesus in the Temple. Each story gives us a picture of a divine child, who behaves in ways typical of and endearing in all children, and yet who inspires awe and cosmic wonder and wisdom. Feelings of indulgence, protection, awe, and wonder toward one's unborn child are common yet very strong in pregnancy. Many mothers are struck, like Mary and Yasoda, by their baby's monumental importance, which throws politics and earthly concerns into a different perspective. A sense of the ultimate significance of this child can be overwhelming and powerful, and is, I think, a sign of the divine spark which forms the soul of each one.

Many women can relate to these sorts of feelings:

The most wonderful thing about becoming a mother is feeling that totally unconditional love, in a way that I have never experienced before.

Emma, eight months pregnant and
mother of a 1-year-old daughter

The most wonderful thing about becoming a mother is the sheer joy and love that you feel for your child, feelings so immense it is difficult to quantify or describe them.

Helen, mother of a 2-year-old son

Small wonder we all feel so emotional at this time!

You might like to reflect on these words if you are feeling overwhelmed:

Tend only to the birth in you and you will find all goodness and all consolation, all delight, all being, and all truth. Reject it and you reject goodness and blessing. What comes to you in this birth brings with it pure being and blessing.

Meister Eckhart

We have already asked what our babies can show us about God. Perhaps the Hindu story and Meister Eckhart's words can add something more to your insights into your feelings about your baby and our world.

Ambivalent Feelings

Sometimes we can feel emotional without really knowing what we are feeling, or why, and sometimes we might feel contrasting things at the same time. As well as joy, a positive pregnancy test might also bring a feeling of "Eek! What have we done?" Many women feel a degree of ambivalence about impending changes of lifestyle and role:

> I was used to doing things when I wanted to do them and had quite a fast pace of life before I had Amy, but now a simple trip to the shop takes lots of planning…I have to wait until she's napping before doing simple things…I have had to learn not to worry…I suppose your priorities just change and things that seemed really important pre-baby don't any more.
>
> *Tess, mother of a 6-month-old daughter*

A well-traveled friend with a successful career put it this way:

> I never dreamed that one day I would be discussing the merits of nipple shields or the best diaper rash cream!
>
> *Harriet, mother of a 10-month-old son*

Thomas Kuhn popularized the concept of a paradigm shift. In his book *The Structure of Scientific Revolutions* he argued that advancement or change is not gradual, but a "series of peaceful interludes punctuated by intellectually violent revolutions." Becoming a parent is a paradigm shift.

Sometimes I feel like I've lost myself completely which is quite frightening. I lived so long as a single independent woman who quite enjoyed being on my own. I have found the whole process of being with someone and being a mother so personally challenging, I have wondered if I can actually do it. Obviously I have, and I do, but sometimes I think nostalgically about the old me.

Hannah, mother of daughters aged 8 months and 2½ years

The thing I have found most challenging about becoming a mother is gaining a new and all-consuming identity that comes with big responsibilities. Having a small person who needs you to nurture them and keep them safe and happy, and having to put them first all of the time. You can't just please yourself any more.

Helen, mother of a 2-year-old son

In these violent revolutions, "one conceptual world view is replaced by another." It takes time and energy to move from one way of being to another, so for a while you will be living in a state of physical and emotional transition, which can be uncomfortable. Adapting to such a big life change is a process—if you are at the beginning of it, give yourself time and allow yourself to go through it rather than feeling that you should already be at the end.

For me, a scene in *The Hitchhiker's Guide to the Galaxy* by Douglas Adams summed it up:

"You'd better prepare yourself for a jump into hyperspace. It's unpleasantly like being drunk."
"What's so unpleasant about being drunk?"
"You ask a glass of water."
Arthur thought about this...

It may be helpful to imagine yourself with a baby rather than yourself as a mother or parent to begin with. These moms draw on their faith to help them adapt to their new role:

This is what God has made a woman to do; nothing is tough, every woman will have in her the natural ability to go through

34

every stage of bearing and raising her baby—and the reward of every hardship I bear will be given to me by God.

> *Robina, mother of a 7-month-old son*

Sometimes I just have to stop and pray and ask God for his grace and wisdom. Being a mother can be so completely all-consuming but I know that I can find strength and peace in God.

> *Jenna, seven months pregnant and mother of a 2-year-old son*

Another mom says:

Have confidence in your ability to be a good mother—if what you're doing feels right it probably is!

> *Rachel, 16 weeks pregnant and mother of five sons*
> *aged between 1 and 8*

And many women find they adapt well to their new role and enjoy the new opportunities and experiences it can bring:

I now have a different set of priorities. It is difficult not having as much time to stay in touch with friends. I don't feel like I've lost friends but I'm not able to spend as much time with them. But now that Hannah is older this is getting easier. I have also met a lot of people as a result of having Hannah and refreshingly people that I might not have met otherwise.

> *Emma, eight months pregnant and*
> *mother of a 1-year-old daughter*

It is encouraging to notice that while many women feel some degree of ambivalence, most find the experience of bringing a new baby into the world to be ultimately satisfying and a source of joy—and most go on to have another. There really is nothing like the feeling of holding your newborn and soaking up each other's gaze. This, I have found, continues: for me there is nothing like sharing a joke with my 11-month-old, and I felt the same seeing his first smile at 6 weeks, and so on. All parents will have their own myriad of little moments—beautiful memories—that leave them glowing.

It seems, then, to be the *process* of change that is uncomfortable, rather than the reason for it or the outcome. In order to appreciate the wonder of this stage of your life in the middle of all sorts of other feelings, it's important to spend some time being fully in the present moment with your new baby or your bump, setting aside other concerns and things to do. Another mom I know confirms this, saying, "Enjoy every moment especially when they are babies because they grow so fast." We can learn from the Buddhist tradition here and Thich Nhat Hanh's book *Peace Is Every Step* starts with a simple but effective meditative exercise to help people to rest in the "present moment, wonderful moment." He also includes a practical tip:

> In my tradition, we use temple bells to remind us to come back to the present moment. Every time we hear the bell we stop talking, stop our thinking, and return to ourselves...whatever we are doing, we pause for a moment.[2]

What might your temple bell be? What might remind you every now and then to just stop and be in the present moment? It could be a regular external sound that brings you back to the here and now, like a clock chiming, your dog barking, the sound of the mail deposited in the mailbox. Or it might be a daily ritual, such as brushing your teeth, having a shower, or drinking your morning coffee. You might like to pin an inspiring quote or picture on the bathroom cabinet or on the 'fridge, to remind you regularly to stop and be still and peaceful.

Your Sense of Your Own Self and Space

Pregnancy and motherhood can bring people inescapably face to face with their own human shortcomings. It can be stressful, and the things many people do to de-stress may not be possible in pregnancy to the same degree. This can heighten our already emotional state to an uncomfortable level. It's time to realize the importance of being kind to yourself and of keeping expectations simple. The same is true when your baby is born. Babies need love and care more than they need a sporty, healthy parent, or a well-read, educated parent for instance (you can add your own hang-ups and challenges here. Maybe there are bad habits you find hard to break, or you feel less affluent than you would like to be. Perhaps you wish your relationship with your partner was better, or that you simply had more energy or maternal feeling.) A child who feels accepted will be accepting back, regardless of how much you might wish yourself to be a new, improved model! Many aspirations for self-improvement are worthy and worth pursuing, but in a spirit of self-acceptance and love, and sometimes with help and support from others. Essentially, though, we are good enough for our babies just as we are when we love them openly.

It's also worth remembering that you are not alone, even though you are in a unique place. I asked a group of new moms what sustains them when the going gets tough. Perhaps you will find this mother's reply helpful to hold onto:

> The thought that on that night the baby is really crying, there are millions of women all over the world going "shhhh, shhhh" and rocking their children just like you are.
>
> *Hannah, with daughters aged 8 months and 2½ years*

If your own sense of self is an area you feel you would like to give some thought to, then pregnancy is an ideal time to develop your sense of positive identity and self-esteem. Paying attention to your inner resources and enhancing positive, accepting thoughts and feelings about yourself can help you to hold onto an innate sense of self-worth during a time of transition. A Quaker phrase refers to "that of God," or "the Light," in each person. Find it in yourself, however you understand it, and find ways of tapping it when you feel in need of nurture and support, or when you feel self-doubt or frustration setting in. There will be times like this with a new baby. Do it out of love for yourself, not just for the love of your child.

It may help you to retain a positive sense of yourself if you can find some physical places and inner places to retreat into. As this mother says:

> What sustains me is having my own space to think and get myself calm if I am feeling cross and tired.
>
> *Vicki, mother of 4- and 6-year-old daughters*

Your Sacred Space

Here are some ideas for finding sacred space.

Physical Places and Internal Spaces

First, try to think of an actual, physical place that is special or sacred to you. What feelings does it evoke when you are there? How do you feel when you leave? Calm, peaceful, refreshed? Maybe more confident? More discerning, with a clearer view or sense of perspective? Relaxed? Energized and ready to deal with whatever life might throw at you? Do you have new insights or a different and unexpected way of seeing things?

Think about the symbols and sacred objects used in places of worship: crosses, flowers, candles, images (e.g., a dove for peace), statues, or of inspirational religious figures (e.g., the Buddha in Buddhist meditation, saints in Christianity). Do you have anything in your space that holds some kind of symbolism for you?

Could you have a shrine of some kind in your sacred space, or objects you could take there when you visit? What might your shrine look like? What would you put on it? What do these objects mean to you and how might they aid inner reflection, memories, meaning, and discernment?

In our home we have what we call the prayer corner with a low table and comfy chair in the bay window of our bedroom. On the table we have some crosses, all decorated differently, which we can pick up and hold; a candle; and some colorful, beautiful plants. Sometimes we add other things—Valentine cards, letters from, or photos of, people we miss or are thinking about. Our positive pregnancy tests were placed there for a while. It's a place each of us can go to for some quiet time. How do you mark your sacred space?

Think about cathedrals and churches, temples, stone circles, or other places that have been or are used in worship. How is the atmosphere enhanced in these different places? In addition to objects that we can see and touch, are there things that appeal to our other senses? Places that leave a lasting impression usually appeal to our senses in a special way. Light, color, decoration, music, silence, echoes, incense, and other smells are all important because of the effect they have on our emotions.

Think about what your special place has that you could hold with you internally when you have to be away from it. That way, by taking a bit of the atmosphere with you, you may be able to access more easily, and in other places, the feelings you have when you are there.

If you don't yet have a sacred space, how might you create one for yourself at home or somewhere you can go when you need to? One place for me is Friar's Crag, overlooking Derwent Water in Cumbria. I used to live nearby, but now I just go there in my mind's eye whenever I want to feel still, calm, and inspired. Another is the middle point on the Gateshead Millennium Bridge in Newcastle-upon-Tyne, where Stephen proposed and we drank champagne...we still live in the area, and when I go there I feel happy and the view back up the river always stirs up some excitement and awe.

In Celtic spirituality, the natural environment and the built environment provide all sorts of sacred spaces. These may be helpful to explore during pregnancy and new motherhood because, as we have seen, there is a link between the natural world, God as Creator, and our own role in the creative process at this time in our lives. Margaret Silf writes about these Celtic ideas in her book *Sacred Spaces*[3]:

- *Hill tops and mountain tops:* These provide a high point and a clear view—things can be seen in perspective and for what they really are. No hiding places!
- *Wells:* The bottom of a well is deep, dark, lonely. But sometimes we have to hit the bottom of the depths in order to find life-giving water and to turn to climb back up again.
- *Bridges:* Bridges connect what might otherwise be divided. They provide access and a path between separated places, people, and feelings.
- *Springs:* Water bubbles up from the ground spontaneously and unexpectedly, nurturing whatever surrounds it and sustaining new life.
- *Clearings in forests or woods:* These are often kept green by the springs. They are places of light and clarity, often to be found or stumbled on after an uncertain walk through obstacles, distractions, or darkness (the forest or wood).

Try to think about how these sorts of places—actual and internal —might be of help to you at the moment. For instance, a new baby might be an internal bridge connecting you more easily to your partner or your in-laws or your own mother. You may feel that you are playing the part of a spring as you nourish the baby. Or perhaps, like me, you too have a real place in a wood or on a hilltop that you go to and which helps you to connect with the Spirit. To help you with this sort of reflective process, you might like to consider some of these questions:

- Why do you think these places in the environment have special significance for people?
- Can you think of any places you know like this?
- Can you think of any spiritual or emotional experiences you have had that might correspond to internal hilltops, wells, bridges, springs, or clearings?
- How might you draw out the significance and effect of these in your life?
- How might you learn to discern such times more often?

Your Symbol

Can you imagine a symbol that could represent yourself at this time in your life, the inner you? The pregnant you? The maternal you?

- What color is your symbol?
- What is it made of?
- What does it feel like to touch?
- Does it move or is it still?
- How do you treat it?
- Have you already befriended it, or do you need to think about doing this? Think about the aspects of yourself that you like the best, and accept your inner self as sacred and valuable.

You could try making your symbol, either in two dimensions using paints, pencils, crayons, or collage, or three dimensionally using found objects, clay, paper, or cardboard. Carry it with you, or add it to your shrine in your special place.

Prayer and How a 4 AM Madonna Might Do It

Many spiritual people might say that when they pray or meditate they are being "the real me"—in prayer or meditation, people can encounter the spiritual in a way that uncovers the different masks they wear. Prayer or meditation can help us to discern God's presence, work, and wishes, so getting to know yourself and being honest about who you are is an important part of prayer. When we are pregnant or looking after a new baby, prayer can help us to feel more centered and to acknowledge and reconcile our feelings. It can give us some much-needed space just to "be" or some time to spend in celebration and thanksgiving. However, it's not always easy with a baby, as this mother points out:

> I don't see how you can go through the process of birth, look at your new baby, and not believe in God. It is what Life is. But I would say I don't have time to meditate!
>
> *Louise, mother of a 1-year-old daughter and a 3-year-old son*

It's important that we are not daunted by the thought of praying regularly, even if we are not sure how to pray, or feel we haven't got much time or much to pray about. I took my new baby to a baby massage class and became friendly with another mother who had a baby the same age as mine. This friend is Muslim, and at her house one day as we were drinking tea she asked if I would help myself to cake for a few minutes because it was time for her to pray and it would only take a couple of minutes. She went off to get her prayer mat. As she prayed in the other room, and I fed my baby, it occurred to me to pray too, so I did. We both know God, and we were both praying at the same time, but in very different styles and as members of different religions. It was a lovely moment, and shows, I think, how varied prayer can be—there are lots of ways of doing it and God can be found through all of them. Sometimes, when we are 4 AM madonnas, we have to be inventive in our prayer lives, as this mother discovered:

> Having a baby makes it harder to have that daily devotion time, and more difficult to worship God during praise and worship

time at church. You have to remember this is just a season and God will honor you. I found I developed a different approach, and simply prayed and spoke with God as I got on with my daily life. This is more attainable and realistic when you're having sleepless nights or have an early riser in the family!

Jane, mother of an 8-year-old daughter and a 5-year-old son

In the next section we'll look at some different ways of praying that may be particularly helpful during pregnancy or when small children are around.

Mantras and Celtic-Style Repetitive Prayers

A *mantra* is a word or phrase that is repeated during prayer or meditation in order to help transcend distractions and intrusions to reach a still, inner center where the Spirit, or self, depending on your spiritual beliefs, can speak and be waited on.

Celtic Christianity dates from a time in the British Isles when new Christian beliefs mingled with local pagan beliefs about the unity of creation, the sacredness of nature, and the divine spark in all living things. Celtic crosses have a circle linking the four parts, representing the oneness of God, the sun which brings light and life, the cycle of life, and the seasons. The crosses are usually decorated with nature-based interlacing patterns, symbolic of the importance and sacredness of the natural world, and a central boss representing either God or the sun as Jesus, Light of the World.

These may be helpful themes to explore in prayer, or images to hold in meditation, while you are pregnant. Celtic prayers reflect these themes and images and are usually written in a simple, soothing, repetitive style. You may also like to hold a Celtic cross or have a picture of one nearby.

If your mind is feeling crowded or if your feelings are overwhelming (both are common states during pregnancy and new motherhood), then praying with mantras or in the repetitive style of Celtic prayers can be calming and soothing. It can allow your intuition or unconscious self some space to surface—and the Spirit a window in. Simply repeat the words out loud or silently, over and over, in quiet and peaceful surroundings, if this is a time of worship, or amid the business of whatever other situation you are in. Keep this up for

A Celtic cross

either a period of time—say, ten or twenty minutes—if you have set aside the time to pray, or just repeat five times, or ten times, as you go if you are busy.

You might like to choose your own mantra—the words may just be given to you. Alternatively, you might find one of the following helpful:

"Calm and relaxed"
"Let your Light shine"
"Lord, be near"
"Come, Jesus"
"New life"
"Rejoice"
"Praise"
"Rest now"

David Adam, formerly vicar of Lindisfarne, has written some profoundly effective yet simple prayers in the Celtic style. Here are two
examples from his book *Landscapes of Light*, which I found helpful
and calming during my pregnancy. I used them when Thomas, my
baby, was tiny, whispering them to him and saying "us" instead of
"me" and "our" instead of "my." I use them again now because,
as I write this book, I have become happily pregnant again. I find
both prayers lovely to fall asleep to, while imagining a circle of light
around the whole family.

Circle me, Lord
Keep protection near
And danger afar

Circle me, Lord
Keep hope within
Keep doubt without

Circle me, Lord
Keep light near
And darkness afar

Circle me, Lord
Keep peace within
Keep evil out.

———➤•◀———

O Lord, Creator of all
Open my Eyes to beauty
Open my mind to wonder
Open my ears to others
Open my heart to you.

Living Prayerfully

There is a lot to do when preparing for a baby, and once the baby is born and the sense of waiting is over, then on the one hand everything slows down and you feel you can't get anything done, but on the other hand, you are busier than you have ever been in your life before—and more tired. Whoever has time to pray, you might ask? If this is true with one baby, it must be even more true with the babies who follow!

Living prayerfully need not always mean setting aside some time each day to pray. It can mean noticing and appreciating moments, the simple things. Even noticing your positive and negative feelings, giving thanks and inviting God in, can be a way of praying. See how short you can make your prayer. Try what I call "clocking prayers." This is when, on a day that is too busy or stressful for anything else, you just "clock" things—that is, briefly notice or acknowledge to yourself anything that helps you to feel good and that you could thank God for, such as service with a smile in a shop, a considerate colleague, a thoughtful action like someone making you a cup of tea, a baby's smile or progress, flowers, a happy event, sunshine, snow, something going right, any small achievement, a chat with a friend. Just clock these things as a form of thanksgiving. Very soon, you will be noticing holy coincidences—the work of the Spirit in your life—just as well as those who have time to pray in more regular ways.

I was wondering how I would ever find time to pray when I came across a really helpful phrase: *therapeutic active prayer*. What a wonderful concept! Activity, particularly that which helps you and your family to live your values and which contributes to your sense of wholeness and well-being, can be prayer. This can include ironing, feeding the baby, cooking for friends, feeding the cat, buying a crib, decorating a nursery, changing a diaper, and dashing to the drugstore for hemorrhoid cream. It can include playing "peekaboo" with your baby and singing "Row, Row, Row your Boat" for the fourth time, with the actions. You just need to be aware of your intentions and motivations—are you turning toward God, or away from God, when you do these things? The beauty of becoming sensitized to the presence of God in everyday life is that the

Spirit can be found, if you look, in everything you do—even the seemingly trivial or frankly boring, providing you are doing it with a sense of its value and of its rightful place in your life, and if you are turning toward God as you do it. God is there to be found in all people, and in all places and situations. If you are reading this thinking, "God is not in my morning sickness," or "God is not in my bank statement," then revisit these assumptions with fresh eyes and just see if you can find something. Might God be sharing what you feel, and in it with you? Might these things be turning you toward God in some way? Following these ideas may lead you to a deeper awareness of God's presence.

Inviting God In

Here are some more ideas for praying. They are all about inviting God in. God has given you this miracle—what will your response be? Few of us are ever 100 percent happy with our prayers, but if we stand back we may notice that God is pleased with any attempt we make to invite the Spirit in and share the experiences and opportunities we have been given. In fact, maybe the recipe for 100 percent successful prayer that will please God entirely is just to *try* to listen and pray? Motherhood is a good chance to deepen your relationship with God in this way. You are loved, trusted, and cherished. Mothers must carry a special place in God's heart because how could God not value those who give themselves to continuing creation?

- My husband keeps two small beads in his pocket. One is dark, the other is light. Each time he puts his hand in his pocket, he is reminded to notice spiritual moments during the day, and also to notice things that are energizing and things that are draining. At the end of the day, he can then give thanks for the former and review how the latter things might have gone differently.

Bella Brown has written:

All our senses are given to us to enjoy, and to praise God. The smell of the sea, of the blossom borne on the wind, of the soft flesh of a little baby; the taste of a ripe plum or bread fresh from the oven, the feel of warm cat's fur, or the body of a lover —these are all forms of thanksgiving prayer.[4]

I think this is the sort of prayer a 4 AM madonna might enjoy. Here are a couple of suggestions:

1 Go on an awareness walk—on your own, with the dog, with your baby. You might just walk round the block, or round a park or your garden, or you might make a trip out into the countryside somewhere. Notice what you see—brickwork, leaves, pebbles, natural things, things that people have made. Notice what you find beautiful, and what jars. As you walk, be open to the Spirit—this is a listening prayer. Take a memento home and build a little collection of finds and memories.

2 Say a senses prayer, either in a room in your house or with your baby. For example:

> I touch your fingers
> I smell your hair
> I see into your eyes
> I listen to your sucking
> I taste your skin when I kiss you
> I feel proud that you are mine. Thank you, Lord.

and:

> I touch the leather of the sofa
> I smell the flowers in the vase
> I see the flames of the fire
> I listen to the CD playing
> I taste the coffee I have sat down here with
> I feel welcome in this room. Thank you, Lord.

The last line of a senses prayer, the "feelings line," may not always be positive. This is OK—acknowledge how you really feel and maybe end with "Be with me, Lord."

- When words are inadequate, or too time-consuming, try just holding someone in the Light for a few seconds in your mind's eye. This sort of prayer doesn't ask for a particular outcome —you are simply (but powerfully) holding someone (and it might be yourself) before God.

- Light a candle for a person or a situation each evening—maybe for an impending birth, or a colicky baby, or a teething toddler, or for yourself and your partner.

- Embody your prayer in an action. When I told my husband we were pregnant, he leapt up and punched the air—this was a thanksgiving prayer in physical form! You may have an interest in yoga or dance, in which case you will already know how a beautiful series of movements can feel spiritual. If you want to experiment, give it a go—make gestures, or put together a series of movements, which suit your prayer. Try this with a written prayer (e.g., the Lord's Prayer, mealtime prayer), or a prayer from a book, or try singing a hymn, chorus, or chant with actions.

- Other ways of praying without words include meditating on nature and meditating on Scripture, each of which give you an external focus. Silent contemplation, on the other hand, involves an inward process of centering down. All can be helpful because they involve listening to God rather than talking, and they can all be done in as much or as little time as you have.

- If you like to pray using words, try using books of poetry or short meditations or prayers, or use your Bible—short extracts are easy to pick up and put down depending on how much time you have, and what you read can influence the direction your prayer takes, whether it is a spoken prayer or simply a period of reflection.

- Use online meditations. These can be beautiful, accompanied by evocative photographs, pictures, and music. Find a quiet moment, maybe light a candle or some fragranced oil, then log on to a meditation and follow it through—you might like to do this daily for a while. They just take a few minutes and can transport you away from the humdrum. I like these Web sites, and they each offer several, changing meditations at any one time: <http://www.interviewwithgod.com> and <http://www.sacredspace.ie>.

- Listen to a piece of music that evokes a particular mood or feeling, and let your mind wander around and dwell on that feeling. You can do this if you already know what you are feeling, or if you are trying to induce a certain mood. Some helpful examples might be:

o Excitement/energy—Mozart, *Eine kleine Nachtmusik*; Iggy Pop, "Lust for Life."

o Anger—Carl Orff, *Carmina Burana*.

o Peace/relaxation—Mozart's Flute and Harp Concerto in C Major; anything by Enya; Norah Jones, "Come Away with Me"; Beethoven, "Moonlight Sonata."

o Wonder/empowerment—Beethoven, "Ode to Joy," from his Ninth Symphony.

o Other atmospheric pieces of music include: Holst, *The Planets*; Allegri's *Miserere*; the theme music to the film *The Color Purple* (from the album *Cinema Serenade*); Norah Jones, "Sunrise" (from the album *Feels Like Home*); Deep Forest, "Sweet Lullaby" (African chant, from the album *Deep Forest World Mix*); the BBC's theme music to *The Blue Planet;* Cat Stevens' album *Tea for the Tillerman;* "Hornpipe" from Handel's *Water Music;* Mozart's *Laudate Dominum;* and Purcell's "Trumpet Tune."

o My husband plays jazz guitar and serenades me with a bathtime medley when I'm pregnant and too tired to do anything other than soak. The selection includes "The Dolphin," "A Child is Born," "My Favorite Things," "A Nightingale Sang in Berkeley Square," "Song for Rachel" (his own composition—lucky me!) and "I'm Forever Blowing Bubbles." No doubt you'll have your own favorites. You can even buy compilations designed for pregnant women and for new babies, but if you know a good musician, get them to serenade you while you put your feet up! Close your eyes, listen to the music, and let your mind wander toward God.

o For those who prefer classical music, there is a great book called *The Harmony of Heaven* by Gordon Giles (see Further Reading), which guides readers through prayer with music during Lent and Easter—and Lent and Easter can be compared to pregnancy and birth as both are times of preparation and waiting followed by new life.

Follow up these times of prayer/reflection/meditation with some of the ideas in the next chapter.

It was the tiniest thing I ever decided to put my whole life into.
Terri Guillemets, author

3

Creative Expression Following Prayer or Reflection

The best thing to spend on your children is time.

Louise Hart, psychologist and educator

After a time of prayer, reflection, or encounter, try to find one or more modes of expression from the range suggested here as a way of recording, completing, or developing your thoughts, feelings, and insights. You might read one idea and be instantly hooked. There may be some suggestions that are already a regular part of your life. Some people may prefer art and drawing, others journaling or storytelling, or maybe music—or, you may just not know until you try a few things. Now is your chance, even if the thought terrifies you! Give some of these ideas a try without any pressure to be good at them—you may be surprised at how powerful they can be if you just go with the flow. I'm eternally grateful to my own spiritual director who encouraged me to try some of these techniques, and I've included some of the results from my journal for you to see.

Creative Drawing

Mandalas

People from many faith traditions use mandalas as a focus for meditation. *Mandalas* are sacred geometric patterns, symbolizing the unity of all things in the universe. The designs can be quite simple or very complex. They have an ancient history, reflected in the circular rose windows of many churches and in the artwork and architecture of Islam, Hinduism, and Buddhism. They encapsulate a beauty and wisdom that have appealed to people making spiritual journeys across the world and across history. By coloring the pattern, many beautiful, different designs can be created. There are specific guidelines for coloring mandalas: start at the center and work outward if the mandala is to bring out and express what is innermost; or start at the edges and work toward the center if the mandala is to help identify and reveal hidden innermost thoughts and feelings. Colors should be chosen instinctively. For some people, colors are intrinsically meaningful or evocative, so the process of choosing a color (or finding a color choosing you) comes naturally and spontaneously. For others, it may take some courage and experimentation—if this is you, explore with a sense of adventure, because you can't go wrong. The finished mandala should be studied thoughtfully and reflectively: what meaning might the colors and patterns have? What do they convey for you? Sometimes the meaning and significance of colors and shapes develops over time and you may need to do a few mandalas to see this emerging.

You can find out more about mandalas at <http://www. mandalaproject.org> and at <http://www.re-xs.ucsm.ac.uk/> (click on World Religions, Art and Pattern for a list of mandala Web sites). The Internet provides access to downloadable mandalas that you can color (try <http://www.free-mandala.com>), and books of outlined designs are available from stationery shops. Try coloring after a quiet period of prayer or reflection.

You could then go one step further and create your own mandala that expresses something meaningful after a time of quiet. Drawing your own mandala is even more powerful than coloring an existing one. Mandalas are always circular and contain symbols, images, shapes, and colors that are unique to the person drawing the mandala. What will you include in yours, and why? Again, work instinctively and without too much analysis—finish your mandala before looking at what it might be saying. I've included some black-and-white reproductions of mine here, with a few words of explanation as it seemed to me at the time.

Many people include symbols and pictures in their mandalas. These may be abstract or more concrete. Do any recur in yours? Color for me is significant—as I have developed my artwork during prayer time I find myself using key colors to symbolize certain feelings or states of mind. These recur through all my mandalas and drawings. As time goes on, if you want to experiment with art in your prayer life, you will come across your own color/feeling combinations—as in chapter 1 of this book. These are some of mine:

Purples/lilacs = peace
Blues = creativity, beauty, transformation
Yellow = God, the light, the Holy Spirit
Red = relationships
Orange = anxiety
Flesh colors = babies

Mandala 1

I drew this mandala (see below) when I was hoping to become pregnant. We were planning to start a family and it was what I wanted most, but I also felt some trepidation. I can see a sense of fun bursting out from this mandala—even the little shapes, which I drew in orange, in the triangles around the edges, look like little figures holding their arms up as if laughing or praising. It conveys a sense of excitement and joy at the thought of having children, as well as a little anxiety. The creative impulse, my own and God's, is there at the center.

Mandala 1

Mandala 2

This extract is taken from my journal, reflecting on this mandala (see page 55), which I drew when I was about five months pregnant:

I think the lilac star symbolizes peace at the center (of me). The green and black symbolize a strong sense of self, despite my recent tiredness.

Green and red triangles—some push out from the center, which is the inner me moving outward. Others point in toward the center: demands and responsibilities from the outside, coming in. The green triangles represent "me," the red ones represent relationships—particularly with the pregnancy and baby. The pattern of the two circles of triangles is disrupted—some of the green ones point out but change to point in, and some red ones are coming in but change to go outward. Pockets of anxiety (orange dots) appear in the gray—I've been feeling a bit overanxious and "grayed out." The green circle shows that my sense of self surrounds this inner tension. The big red triangles pointing out from the green circle show that my relationship with the pregnancy/baby is strong. The big green triangles pointing in from outside are the parts of me, the things I enjoy, the aspects of life that I have enjoyed so far, which are being broken into by this new relationship—pockets of anxiety again about this. I'm giving up or changing a familiar lifestyle and aspects of myself are being tested, maybe changed, maybe sacrificed, for a relationship that I desire but do not yet fully know or have. Something that I know is fulfilling is being pushed through, broken into, by something which I hope will be fulfilling but do not know. I can only risk and trust.

Yellow = the presence of God in this process, there as a backdrop and shining through, linking it all together. All of this is circled by the baby (flesh color).

From this I went on to record what I felt I needed most in the light of my feelings. This included self-kindness—time for reflection and fun and to do a range of things I enjoyed. I also felt I needed to read encouraging books and articles written by people who had made successful and enjoyable transitions into motherhood, and to spend time with friends who were enjoying new parenthood but still managing to retain those other parts of life and self-identity that they enjoyed, people for whom new family life was enhancing

Mandala 2

rather than replacing what they found fulfilling. My journal entry finished with:

I feel very aware of how lucky I am. My journey here feels both discerned and guided. I have sought for and found the right partner, the right place. I need have no anxieties about my sense of self disintegrating in this change—it could be life unfolding with even more abundance.

"Less-Preferred-Hand" Drawings

Ideally, less-preferred-hand drawings are best done after a time of private inner reflection rather than public worship, and at a time when you are prepared for your doodles to reveal some deep subject matter—it's an exercise that can tap the subconscious very effectively. The technique involves taking a pencil and eraser, and without too much thought drawing freehand on a plain piece of paper with the hand you do *not* normally use. So, if you are right-handed, use your left hand for this. Let your hand go where it will. This exercise creates the opportunity for your body to express something in its movement that is meaningful and important in the present. Letting go and seeing what happens can be likened to allowing a new creation to be born.

Sit back and look at the lines and the shapes you have made. Sometimes an image or design will spring out at you straight away; at other times you may need to look more closely, or rotate the paper. Use the pencil and eraser to clarify the lines and shapes you want to keep and to erase what isn't needed. You can add color or not, as you choose.

What do you have?

- Is the image on the paper a revelation and surprise, or a summary of what you have been reflecting on?
- Is there anything you need to do—a conversation you need to have, or a course of action to take—as a result of this?
- If you can't see anything at all, just put the paper aside and try the exercise again another time. I don't see things every time. I find when it works it can be a powerful exercise but one best done less frequently than the others suggested in this section.

Here are three of my own examples of the exercise working well.

Left-Handed Drawing 1: Motherhood
This first one (page 57) is particularly interesting to me because I could see in it a clearly maternal image. The larger, outer shape, drawn in blue, looks to me like a mother cradling and bending over the smaller, internal figure, which I shaded in fleshy tones. I drew this using these techniques when I was just a few days pregnant—I didn't know it at the time as it was too early for me to tell, but something in my psyche knew!

Left-Handed Drawing 2: Swan and Cygnet
This second image (page 58) was made a couple of months into the pregnancy. The image of a swan carrying a cygnet across the water just jumped off the page from among a lot of other lines that I erased. The green shape, which I interpreted as myself, reminded me of a swanlike figure gliding forward with another figure, the peachy colored cygnet, on its back, riding in the same direction. I think it's a very serene and intimate, self-contained image.

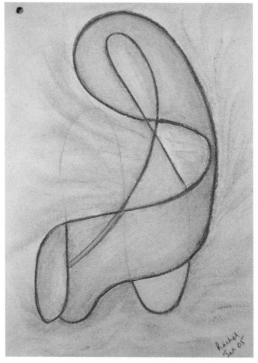

Motherhood

Left-Handed Drawing 3: Mother and Baby Ball

The third image (page 59) strikes me as a bit comical. It seems to be only in my less-preferred-hand drawings that images of actual characters—people or animals—emerge, rather than geometrical shapes or wavy patterns. They are also the only pictures I name and give titles to. The shape of this little creature is reminiscent of a mandala. In my notes I wrote:

> This is the inner me (green) and the baby (flesh-colored) clinging onto each other as we spin, hurtle, or rotate through space and time. Part of me is looking back to my previous life and familiar things, part of me is holding onto or joined to the baby. Themes: embracing the new/inner tensions/conflicting but positive elements in life/looking back or hanging onto "now" while heading toward a changing future.

Swan and cygnet

Although it reflects some of the uncomfortable sensations that can come with major changes and transitions, I think this is a happy image because the baby and I are very much attached to each other, and we're moving forward together as a team.

Free-Flow Patterns

Drawing free-flowing patterns after a time of prayer or reflection, or even after a time of activity or a specific encounter, can be soothing and expressive, and also insightful. Drawing free-flow patterns simply involves taking some colors and a piece of paper and following your intuition. You don't need to be able to draw. Just go with the flow and make whatever patterns, marks, shapes, and squiggles you feel like, in whatever colors catch your eye. Create different textures as the mood takes you. Literally, go with the flow. It's an abstract thing!

Afterward, you could consider:

- How does the act of drawing the patterns make you feel? What effect on your mood did the exercise have?
- What might the patterns, colors, shapes, flow, and textures reveal or express?

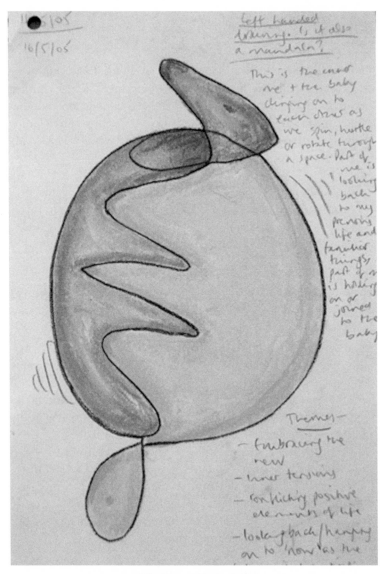

Mother and baby ball

Some examples of my own follow.

Free-Flow Pattern 1

This doodle (page 61) was done after a lovely meal and good wine one evening with my husband (then my fiancé), and I think it captures a light-hearted mood. We had been talking, among other things, about our wedding plans and also our desire to start a family fairly soon afterward, wondering when or if we would be lucky. My journal entry after drawing this pattern reads:

> I'm feeling silly, relaxed, quirky. I'm enjoying thoughts of having children/conceiving. There is a feeling of spring in this pattern—in me, and as a symbol of fertility, lightness, joy, and hope. The yellow and white symbolize the Spirit, God, light.

Free-Flow Patterns 2 and 3

These patterns (page 62) were made over a year later, toward the end of my pregnancy. The colors (not reproduced here) I used are significant for me: purples and lilacs symbolize peace; yellow and white symbolize God. Blue is creativity, beauty, and transformation; greens are the real inner me; and reds and pinks symbolize my relationships. I use black to represent depth of feeling, rather than particularly negative feelings. The shapes seem organic—the circles remind me of ovum and wombs, the wavy lines of the flow of life and the journey babies make from conception to birth.

I think the lines, shapes, and different textures are interesting, and they inspire different responses in me each time I look at them. I didn't write anything down after drawing these patterns, and sometimes it can be helpful not to define them too closely because then the picture can be used in the future as a meditative tool and evoke a different atmosphere each time.

- What sort of response do these patterns inspire in you?
- What feelings are evoked as you let your eyes trail over these patterns?

Free-flow pattern 1

Collage

Fantasy Files and "Discovery Journals"

Some years ago I went through a phase of making three-dimensional collages, using images cut out from magazines and sticky little fixing pads. This is a striking way to build a picture, quite aside from prayer time, but what struck me in the end was how I chose what to cut out. Sometimes I looked for specific things, but usually I chopped out anything that interested me, without querying too much, and I kept everything in a file for later. When I wanted to do a collage, I would have a range of images there to choose from to make up my picture. This was my "fantasy file." Melissa Hill, author

Free-flow pattern 2

Free-flow pattern 3

of *The Smart Woman's Guide to Staying at Home*, uses a similar technique more reflectively:

> I keep a large artist's sketchpad for my Discovery Journal and will occasionally flip through magazines cutting out pictures of anything capturing my fancy. The pictures or phrases can be glued into the journal randomly...or you can group them by theme. Either method gives you a page of appealing images to meditate on whenever you need inspiration. The Discovery Journal allows you safely and privately to examine your interests, desires, and cravings...The Discovery Journal has allowed you to create a symbolic picture of who you really are.

Scrapbooks

Keep photos, cards, letters, quotes, thoughts, and pictures of your own, summaries of holidays or outings, favorite comfort food recipes, reviews of books read during your pregnancy, ultrasound scan pictures, and mementos of special occasions, all pasted into a large and colorful informal scrap book as a "work in progress" testament to your family's life. Start a new one for your baby when he or she is born. A friend of mine did this, and designed a front cover that read, "One Year of Christopher—Thank You for Making Us Smile ☺!"

Creative Writing

There are many ways of using personal writing to enhance your spiritual life. Here are just a few suggestions that might be well suited to this particular time.

Keep a Traditional Journal

Record your encounters, experiences, thoughts, and feelings. Write in the first person and store your book privately if you don't want others to read it. Journal writing can be a therapeutic exercise to try during times of transition such as pregnancy and early parenthood. Reread sections of it yourself periodically, such as at the end of each month, so that you can discern movement and patterns, meaning, and priorities from your record.

Short Stories

These can take many forms and the subject matter is endless. As you are pregnant, why not retell or dramatize with a little artistic license stories from your own family's history or from your own experiences in life so far (e.g., from your childhood), and create a set of unique story books for your child?

Songs

An earlier section invites you to try writing your own Magnificat. Why not also try identifying two key feelings that are around for you at the moment, and a key event that you have experienced. Write simple songs about each of them, conveying to a rhythm or pattern what they are like.

Babies love to be sung to. Sing your baby's name and experiment with simple tunes and the sort of sweet nothings new parents say to their babies. Make it up as you go along, telling your baby some of the beautiful things you want him or her to hear. If you are not so musical, simply try tapping out the rhythm as you say the songs aloud, and add actions. "Kiss the baby," "It's wonderful you, just wonderful you," and "Amazing baby" might be good phrases to try to a tune.

If you're making up rhymes for children about different feelings, you could take as your inspiration a well-known song such as "If you're happy and you know it, clap your hands…" and adapt it: "If you're sleepy and you know it, blink your eyes…If you're sleepy and you know it, hang your head…," "If you're angry and you know it, stamp your feet/wear a frown…," and so on. Advertising jingles and pop songs can be a good starting point too. Kylie Minogue sings "I should be so lucky…"—can you use a snappy tune and change the words to suit your mood?

Songs written for yourself may be more like poems and can provide, through rich use of metaphor, simile, and other literary devices, a broad canvas for exploring the full range of emotions and experiences. Poems like this do not need to follow a format, but some popular formats are suggested next for those who might want to try them.

Different Forms of Poetry

I've always enjoyed poetry—reading it and writing it—but when I ran the following ideas past some friends, their reaction reminded me of a bit in *The Hitchhiker's Guide to the Galaxy*, which says: "The prisoners sat in the Poetry Appreciation chairs—strapped in ...!" However, fear not, and please continue—you might like it! So far, a lot of the things I've suggested have been visual—the ideas in this section are more literary and musical, which you may find suit you just fine.

Try using time of quiet reflection or prayer, or a story, a guided visualization, or a picture as a stimulus.

Haikus

Haikus are Japanese poems made up of 17 syllables in total, usually divided into three lines. You could use this example to help you to write your own.

> baby safe inside
> part of me yet separate
> its own little self

Septains

Septains are poems with seven lines where the first line is one word, the second two, then three, then four, then back to three, then two, and finally one. Copy the format below and have a go.

> Mother
> of God
> cradles her child
> while the stars shine
> then dreaming again
> 4 AM Madonna
> sleeps

Cinquaines

Cinquaines are five-line poems with twenty-two syllables: two syllables, four syllables, six, eight, two. The first line is a noun, the second line is two adjectives that describe the noun, the third is three verbs, the fourth is a phrase of four words, and the fifth is a synonym of the first noun. Again, copy this format and give it a try.

Newborn
awake, eager
to touch, to feed, to gaze.
Tender loving mother hurries,
infant.

Magnetic Poetry

You can buy sets of magnetic poetry—a box of hundreds of words to stick to your 'fridge—and they can be great fun. Try to resist just using these to leave messages for other members of your household! Play around as you drink your coffee or tea, and involve your children as they get bigger. After prayer time, pick a handful of words that describe your encounter and see what you can do with them.

Stream of Consciousness

Here you just write, on a given topic or just on whatever you find yourself writing about. Give yourself a time scale, such as two minutes, and rather like the free-flow patterns earlier, just go with the flow. Don't bother with punctuation, or even a proper writing style unless you want to or need to—just write. This is a great way to vent strong feelings and to express yourself in an uninhibited way, which you might not do verbally. You may not want to leave your paper lying around for others to see. This strategy can tap your subconscious in a similar way to drawing with your less-preferred hand, so expect some surprises, and be prepared afterward to need to think through whatever comes up and take appropriate action if necessary.

Letters

When you are pregnant and when your baby has been born, why not write letters to him or her and keep them safe for the future —a great eighteenth birthday present, and a great way of keeping in touch with your feelings, thoughts, hopes, and dreams about the baby through a sea of morning sickness and diapers.

Sensory Imaging

Sensory imaging requires no tools such as pens or paper. You do need to be comfortable and relaxed, and to have some peaceful time to yourself. You might like to try a stilling exercise first—either listening to some music or being mindful of your breathing, or simply sit and relax each part of your body in turn. Focus on your breath, making it slow, deep, and regular.

You might like to try one or all versions of this exercise.

- *Imagine a future situation*—being in the hospital for the baby's delivery, 4 AM with a newborn sometime after that, or walking in a park with your toddler in a few years' time. For me, imagining Thomas playing with his as yet unborn sibling is powerful —so is imaging the change from being the parent of one child to being the parent of two. Close your eyes and try to imagine what you might see, hear, smell, taste, touch, and feel. Spend some time there, building up the mental image and imagining you really are there, absorbing through your senses as much as you can to make the experience as real as possible.

  Notice how you feel. Where the images cause apprehension, replace these sensory perceptions with familiar and comforting ones. For example, when I imagined Thomas' birth (and early in my third trimester I found the thought quite overwhelming), I imagined I could see the color orange, which for me represents anxiety. In fact, parts of the maternity ward really were painted orange, I noticed on my tour, which at the time did nothing to ease my fear of hospitals, medical procedures in general, and gynecological ones in particular! So I replayed the scene, wrapping a peaceful lilac around the orange, and imagined the baby being handed to me in a soft, lavender-scented lilac blanket (I actually bought one and took it into the hospital with me and requested that this happen). I imagined sprinkling lavender essential oil on my pillow in the hospital to remind me of home. Which colors, smells, tastes, sights, and textures do you find most comforting?
- *Choose a Bible story.* The annunciation might be a good one to try at this time (see Luke 1:26–38), or Sarah's story in the

A story about life and birth, creation and creating

Imagine how you were before you were born...
As you close your eyes and feel the darkness surround you,
stretch before you and enclose you, imagine the void before
creation...you are floating in darkness and love....

PAUSE and reflect, using all your senses.

Imagine birth! Imagine standing at the beginning of time as
the first day explodes into being with a flash of beautiful light
...the new colors and sounds swirl around you, catching you
up in an ever-unfolding universe of light
and love...

PAUSE and reflect, using all your senses.

Imagine now the rising waters of the second and third days,
the waves and ripples, the circles on the surface of blue
oceans and silver lakes...clouds floating in the new clear sky
...Notice the colors of dry land as the countries appear...
deserts and mountains...forests and beaches...Your new world
is taking shape...you are taking shape...

PAUSE and reflect, using all your senses.

Imagine standing on earth on the fourth day and looking out
into the vastness of space as the first stars start to twinkle...
Notice standing under the first sun, feeling the first rays of
warmth on your skin...Notice the first full moon as it lights up
the beautiful night sky...you are experiencing the wonder of
the infinite...and marveling at your
special place in it...

PAUSE and reflect, using all your senses.

Imagine the wonder of the fifth day, as the oceans fill up with
fish all the colors of the rainbow, all shapes and sizes...Marvel

at the majesty of the first blue whale, the clown fish darting in front of you, the penguins and the leaping salmon...Imagine hearing the first-ever bird song, and seeing the bright colors of the first parrots and humming birds...where would you fly to if you were a bird? Do you feel that the world is your oyster? Where will you find your special pearls...?

PAUSE and reflect, using all your senses.

Imagine walking through the Garden of Eden as the first animals are created...Which would you most like to see? Which to you would be the most exciting...? The most frightening...? The most lovable...? Notice how you feel as you see the first zebra...the first kitten...the first dinosaur...You are exploring your new world...What will you contribute to it...?

PAUSE and reflect, using all your senses.

Imagine meeting a brand-new person, a new creation ...What do you imagine them to look like...? To sound like...? Where do you want to take them...? Do you have questions to ask them...? What message would you like to give them...? Imagine you have created this new person... What do you want them to know...? What can you whisper in their ear...?

PAUSE and reflect, using all your senses.

Imagine now feeling tired...the first week of life has passed and you have seen it all, tasted it all, touched it all, smelt it all, and heard it all...You are alive! As you rest in the shade, which day do you feel most grateful for...? Which of your five senses are you most grateful for...? Reflect on your own impending and creative birth experience...and notice how you feel as you rest.

Hebrew Scriptures (see Genesis 18:1–15 and 21:1–7). Follow the same technique. Close your eyes and try to imagine what you might see, hear, smell, taste, touch, and feel. Spend some time there, building up the mental image and imagining you really are there, absorbing through your senses as much as you can to make the experience as real as possible. When working with a story in this way, you might like to see if your imagination gives you a part to play—do you become one of the characters, or are you an onlooker? Can the people in the story see you and talk to you, or are you an invisible visitor from another dimension? What is it like if you allow yourself to enter the scene as a pregnant woman, or as a mother with a young baby? Are you welcomed? Respected? What do people say to you? How do they look at you?

- *Read or listen to a guided visualization,* or record your own imaginative retelling of a story that has a significant subject. It seems to me that the Genesis creation story retold in this way might be powerful when one is busy in pregnancy creating one's own new life, or tending to the needs of a newborn. My own version of this is shown on pages 68 and 69. This could be done in a group setting, for example at an antenatal group, with one person reading thoughtfully and conducive music playing in the background. Some opportunity for sharing afterward would work well, or if you do this alone, spend some time afterward with your thoughts and maybe your journal.

The pursuit of truth and beauty is a sphere of activity in which we are permitted to remain children all our lives.

Albert Einstein, physicist

4

Where Do We Find Our Support and Inspiration?

It is easy to find books, magazines, and Web sites that aim to support pregnant women and new parents, and these have their role—particularly in terms of providing information and chat. However, I became infuriated at the medicalization of the whole experience and at the lack of resources aiming to help women to explore the new landscape on an emotional and spiritual level. In fact, most shy away from doing so, merely mentioning the "baby blues" as inevitable and advising aromatherapy baths and frozen casseroles when the going gets tough. Not enough! Some resources trivialize the process and in doing so deny women the opportunity and resources to fully engage with the paradigm shift they are part of. I did not feel depressed, but I did want to dwell on and explore my feelings through the whole experience. I was in a new phase in life, which meant a small new person depended on me for imaginative support and inspiration, and I needed to find that for myself too. I found these words encouraging:

> In everyone's life, at some time, our inner fire goes out. It is then burst into flame by an encounter with another human being. We need to be thankful for those people who rekindle the human spirit.
>
> *Albert Schweitzer, theologian*

So I started to look for my own people who might provide a flame.

Who Inspires, and Why?

Like it or not, your baby will be fundamentally shaped and formed by you. One mother says:

> I know what I give and teach my baby today will be passed to generations to come, even when I am long gone.
> *Robina, mother of a 7-month-old son*

We all hope that what our babies receive, what they take in, will be inspiring and life-giving. It's a scary thought, but crumbling under the weight of this responsibility, or ignoring it altogether, are not the best responses. Let yourself depend on people who have inspired you, and find new sources of inspiration to help you through this new phase in your life. Let yourself take them in, and let them shape you. Part of your role as a new mother is to let all the goodness inside you flow out into your relationship with your baby. So let yourself be an inspiration, rather than being filled with self-doubt or slavishly following baby care rule books—parent with your heart, and ensure your heart has on call all that has inspired it. As they grow, help your children find other sources of inspiration too, so that at each stage of their journey they are supported and able to find the wisdom they need to develop into themselves.

Pregnancy and new motherhood can be a great time for exploring new ideas—because all your old assumptions are being challenged. But finding the most helpful sources of support and inspiration can be a journey in itself. In this chapter I will refer to a few of the things I discovered on my journey and suggest some ways in which you might get started.

A wise member of my Quaker meeting often quotes George Fox as a source of inspiration, helping him to remain inspiring for younger members of the meeting in modern times. This is one of my favorite quotes from George Fox[2]:

> Be patterns, be examples in all countries, places, islands, nations, wherever you come, that your carriage and life may

preach among all sorts of people, and to them; then you will come to walk cheerfully over the world, answering that of God in every one (AD 1656).

More simply, he also said, "Let your lives speak," but I like the advice to "be patterns." It's what parents are to their children, and I think parents are also in the business of helping children to work out what they want their pattern to be and to explore ways in which they might develop it—while being aware that the process carries on well into adulthood for most of us. No small challenge!

During my first pregnancy Pope John Paul II died. I remember being struck by the enormous variety of people *outside* the Roman Catholic Church who were genuinely saddened by his death, and respectful. His funeral was attended by representatives and leaders of a wide range of world faiths. Even the media, while not being shy about engaging with the debate about the effects of conservative Roman Catholic leadership, seemed on the whole to reflect a certain pronounced respect for John Paul II himself. Tony Blair commented that the "world [has] lost a religious leader who was revered across people of all faiths and none." I began to wonder what it was about this person who could inspire so many people who did not actually share all of his beliefs and philosophies, or follow his teaching. There seems to have been something about his pattern of personal faith and bearing that gave him a quiet dignity and humility, which commanded respect even among disparates, and which drew people, crossing diversity and bridging ideology—for a while, at least. I cannot think of many leaders, religious or secular, who can do this.

In psychological terms, the concept of the self is important, as it is in Christianity, too. Both are concerned with the real person. Therapists work with people to help them to build their self-esteem, or their compassion, acceptance, and mindfulness, to develop a strong sense of identity. In Christianity, "I" am a unique individual, created by God with a unique soul. However, despite the importance attached to the individual in both psychotherapy and Christianity, the two are often held in tension. In the therapist's room, an individual grows to recognize a sense of self so that it can be supported, developed, defended, nurtured. In churches, an individual grows to recognize a sense of self so that it can be sacrificed or offered up in Christian service—self-sacrifice, or martyrdom, is a virtue. When I was younger and beginning to be interested in both psychology and religion, I found this a very difficult tension. Should I be finding myself, or losing myself, I wondered? I was tremendously grateful to be introduced to Ignatian spirituality and to the idea that our deepest desires are of God. I also grew to a more mature understanding of what Christianity might be saying: that "I," "me," and "you" are all labels that describe unique, created individuals, but that an egotistical sense of self-importance might be better sacrificed. My understanding of psychotherapy also involves the idea that bringing someone to a whole and healthy sense of who they really are might mean sacrificing some unhelpful assumptions about one's self.

When we think about who inspires us, we are in part thinking about who that person is inside—the "I," and also about the self that "I" presents to the world. But perhaps neither Christianity nor psychology has the whole understanding: a person is a combination of the two and also so much more. A person is more than the sum of his or her parts. Self-awareness or self-consciousness is limited by what we know or experience within ourselves, whereas personhood —being a unique individual—entails relationship, and as soon as we are drawn into relationship (from being conceived in the womb ourselves, to conceiving our own child), we are already embarking on a journey that will have ramifications more subtle than we can know. This is our pattern in the world. For this reason, a person can have an effect on other people and on the world in a way that they may never know or fully realize or be able to explain. Often, where famous people or public figures are concerned, biographers can have a deeper insight into who the person was. But ordinary people too can be more than they know themselves to be and more than either psychology or religion encourages them to recognize themselves to be. We inspire when we really get to the heart of who we are, and we are inspired when we really get into the heart of someone else. The effect we have on others, and the effect they have on us, can be tremendous. One mother I know talks about the profound effect her aunt has had on her, feeling that she has achieved more and inspired others more than she will ever know:

She is one of my best friends and one of the most supportive and loving people I have ever met. If I can achieve one tenth of what she has in the last twelve years I will be a better person as a result of it.

Tracey, mother of an 8-month-old daughter

It can be helpful to give some thought to how and why people inspire, and also to the role of prayer, meditation, and faith, and the effects these have on the "carriage and life" of many inspiring people. For Christians, the key relationship that brings us to true life and inspiration is with God. Inspiration cannot be separated from outcome. How are we patterns? Which virtues and values inspire you, and to do what? How can we reflect this in family life? We are often inspired by people we depend on. "In-spire" refers to what you "breathe in." You can be certain that your baby will be absorbing you in a fundamental and formative way, breathing you in deeply, daily. By thinking about who and what you allow to inspire you, you will be preparing yourself to be a good pattern for your children. Pregnancy is a time of waiting and preparation before receiving the gift of a child—it is also a time of waiting and preparation before your child receives the gift of you.

Jungian psychoanalyst Clarissa Pinkola Estés writes in her book *Women Who Run With the Wolves*,[3] from a feminine perspective, about the importance of ordinary people who inspire:

Even if you had the most wonderful mother in the world, you may eventually have more than one. As I have often told my own daughters, "You are born to one mother, but if you are lucky, you will have more than one. And among them all you will find most of what you need." Your relationships with *todas las madres*, the many mothers, will most likely be ongoing ones, for the need for guidance and advisory is never outgrown, nor, from the point of view of women's deep creative life, should it ever be.

This part of her book recalled for me the numerous inspiring figures I have met along the way—often women, but not exclusively. I can list them all and still feel indebted to their wisdom, discernment, and challenge, which each offered at the right time and in the right place to help me to develop and become more "me." This made me wonder if I feature in anyone else's list, and, if I do, what my contribution might have been. As I prepared for the birth of my baby, thinking about the people who have inspired me and noticing their effect in my life was particularly meaningful. It helped me to consider the ways in which I hope I can inspire a special new life on a new journey. Maybe you might find it helpful to think back over your own life or spiritual journey so far, and list those who have been significant in this way. Can you identify the qualities in each person that you found inspiring? Where now in your own home life or outside in your community life might your children find these qualities? How might you be able to help them to recognize values and develop qualities that will inspire, encourage, and support them?

For many new moms, the people they meet regularly provide quite astonishing inspiration. When I asked one new mom about who inspires her, she came up with two very real and very different examples. I think both are poignant:

> My yoga teacher—she had her baby four months after me and she can put her legs over her head! I also think of another friend who had IVF [in vitro fertilization] triplets and who lost her husband to cancer when they were only 3 months old. If I need inspiration, I only need to remind myself of her situation.
>
> *Harriet, mother of a 10-month-old son*

Another mom offers this advice:

> I found it really helped in the early days of becoming a mom to get to know other people in the same situation—peer support is really important.
>
> *Rachel, 16 weeks pregnant and*
> *mother of five sons aged between 1 and 8*

And this mom also draws on her friends for inspiration:

> My Christian friends who are moms too inspire me—especially the ones who have children that bit older—it's great to know

people who know what you're going through and who have come out the other side with happy, well-balanced children.

Jenna, 7 months pregnant and mother of a 2-year-old son

Stories and Desires

In terms of external influences, stories can be powerful in reflective periods of life. Stories can have the power to reveal and to help us to explore the diversity in aspects of feminine experience such as birth and motherhood. Clarissa Pinkola Estés' book takes a sample of folk tales and unpacks them in terms of their meaning for the female psyche. Her analysis of the mother duck and exiled duckling motifs in "The Ugly Duckling" offers fascinating insights into how mothering can sometimes go wrong, and in doing so, points to ways in which we can all regain our inner and outer sense of rightness: "for when one develops adequate strength—not perfect strength, but moderate and serviceable strength—in being oneself and finding what one belongs to, one can then influence the outer community and cultural consciousness in masterful ways." How do we gain this strength? By allowing our own internal mother, which is a legacy from our actual mother, to be nurtured and developed, and also through investing in our own unique creativity: "do your art," and "It is never a mistake to search for what one requires." If you are lucky enough to have a strong legacy from your own mother, this will be easier, but it may be all the more important if your legacy is a broken one.

Margaret Silf, in her book *Inner Compass*, includes the exercise of picking one's favorite childhood fairy tale and looking at its components with reference to our own dreams, desires, hopes, and experiences. She says:

> Fairy tales take us right to the heart of our desiring by way of pictures, symbols, and metaphors, and help us to connect these deep and universal desires (and fears) to the feelings we are experiencing in our own particular circumstances.[4]

My favorite story as a small child was Cinderella—despite the feminist I became as a teenager! Margaret Silf calls this a "becoming who I really am" story, so even though I still love romance and fabulous clothes, there is clearly more to it than that. Looking back now with adult eyes, I can see in this choice of reading a great deal to do with my own childhood feelings of wanting to be pretty and accepted, of wanting to escape (school, at that point), of wanting to meet my own soulmate one day, and about the importance of my own grandmother (the godmother figure). Today, I would still count it as central to my happiness to be accepted and loved, and also to be free to be independent from the mainstream. I know I feel less happy when I do not have these things, and perhaps they are fairly universal desires, or perhaps yours are different. While I was pregnant I spent some time exploring my deepest desires, as Saint Ignatius recommends. I finally defined them as:

1 Close supportive relationships, loving and affirming, equal and honest—with Stephen, with family, and friends. Extending a reflection of this to all I meet.
2 Beauty, creativity, and transformation—making a difference. Within this I include discernment of spiritual values and different ways of exploring and expressing the light of God, the life-giving Spirit.
3 Freedom within a safe place to be truly me, and to explore and express what this means, unfettered by imperatives from outside—independence of mind and spirit.

These deepest desires are what I need in order to feel happy, "me," and close to God. I am fortunate enough now to have a life in which they are all fulfilled, so they are not desires in the sense of wanting something I don't have, but in the sense of discerning how I want to live. Now that I have had one baby and I am expecting another, if I did this exercise again there would be another desire around having my own children, and experiencing the joy that getting to know them and spending time with them can bring. My own family life and home life has become a central desire. I remember feeling like a light had gone on in my head when I realized that our own deepest desires might also be God's desires for us, not at all selfish and so not to be sacrificed or ignored, but to be sought and nurtured.

Revisiting a favorite childhood story and thinking about it in these terms—that is, in terms of what it can reveal about hopes, dreams, and desires—also helped me to realize the importance of trying to identify what my own child might need and feel, and of being open to and accepting of these feelings and needs.

If you like reading, make it your own task to find encouraging literature that works for you, and try turning to classical children's stories to search for new messages or insights now that you are an adult. My own parents encouraged my imagination and inspired a love of reading in me that will enrich my life forever. Consider which stories you would like to read to your child, and why.

Manuals and Experts—Discerning Our Way

One book that I have found to be particularly interesting is *The Continuum Concept: In Search of Happiness Lost* by Jean Liedloff. It's a controversial book. Her observations and theories, based on her time with the Yequana people of South America, underpin a lot of the attachment-parenting ideals. She writes about how our lives—as a species and individually—are part of a long-established continuum that modern Western society tends to break, with ill effects. Recognizing the continuum and finding ways to honor it for our children today provides a key to happiness, she argues. I found this a really helpful image as I read some parenting books that offered, it seemed to me, horrific advice which went against my every instinct of how I wanted to treat my baby and of what sort of child I hoped we would enjoy living with. Some people don't enjoy reading parenting books, but if you do, then you may be aware of the completely different positions they can take on what might seem to be fundamental issues. Seek to be inspired, rather than instructed. In terms of offering advice, what parenting books have done is to step into the vacuum left by extended families and community living, which today are sadly often absent or remote. However you choose to parent needs to fit in with your overall values. What I say here about parenting books relates to my own experience—take some time to discover yours for yourself.

I realized that many baby books seem to me to adopt a formula and apply it regardless of any baby's individual personality, and it's often a formula devised originally for older children with established difficulties. It's also often a formula motivated primarily by enabling adults to sleep through the night again as soon as possible and generally sooner than babies are designed to do so. I think it might be more sensible to help new parents to adapt their lifestyle, as adults can, in order to understand and accommodate a new person and to meet their specific needs with a large degree of self-lessness. Babies are not convenient; we notice they have arrived and that they have needs, which we have to make sacrifices to meet. We cannot hope to carry on our lives as normal and simply "slot them in." But the rewards are great if the approach is generous and warm and open to all these changes. William and Martha Sears write, in *The Fussy Baby Book:* "For the sake of your child, and yourself, in the early weeks of parenting, unload the baggage of your 'control mind-set' and learn to give freely." Becoming a mother has been the most rewarding thing I have ever done, but if I had approached it all differently and tried to resume life as I knew it and make my baby more convenient, I would have ended up resenting him and losing myself. This doesn't mean I haven't also found it hard at times. Some women find it helpful to put some time aside to grieve for their old life, rather than waiting for the day when they get their old life back. They recognize that they have a new life evolving, which includes their baby—it does not have to be a power battle of wills.

However, there can be little recognition in some parenting books that a new baby may be allowed to change your life to that of a parent, and has different needs than a crawling baby, who again has different needs than a toddler. The continuum is not recognized, and so our children's and our own primal expectations for each stage of our development are often not met. At the time of writing, there is a trend for feeding schedules, sleep training, and for using controlled crying methods to correct a baby. However, I think such ideas miss the point, that whereas an older child can be shaped, a baby *needs* to be fed and *needs* to sleep or be awake at times that may change from day to day and that may not seem convenient to, or easy for, his or her parents. To apply the strategy of controlled crying to young babies simply teaches them that their desperate cues—and the only way in which they can communicate what they need—are hopeless because they will not have any effect. Some may bounce back unscathed, but others can get resigned to feeling "not OK" and they can disengage, disheartened. Some shout all the louder for the slightest reason to ensure they are heard because they can't rely on a normal request generating a normal response. This may have long-term effects. Writer Deborah Jackson, in her book *Three in a Bed*, renames controlled crying "learned helplessness." It also trains a mother to ignore her natural instincts, some of which are physiological (e.g., your baby's cry can trigger your milk letdown). Your baby's cry has a specific effect on *your* hormones and *your* emotions, which only you can feel and respond to. Honoring this is, in my experience, more fulfilling than ignoring it. Parenting author and former nurse Pinky McKay writes: "Your baby's cry has been designed for her survival and you are programmed to react....by not responding to your baby's signals, the only things being 'spoilt' are your relationship with your baby and your own self-confidence." (This quote comes from an article called "Cuddle Me Mum" on her Web site <http://www.bellybaby.com.au/articles/baby/cuddle-me-mum.)

New babies do demand your constant time, physical presence, and emotional energy—it can be very hard, but this period is short and babies are not manipulative, just dependent. Our society values independence, so having someone so dependent on us may not always feel very comfortable. Yet, in Jesus we see how important *inter*dependence is. He forms bonds with the needy and depends on others for support and friendship (see Luke 8:1–3). In contemporary Western culture, a baby's normal healthy attachment is often confused with insecurity or even insatiability because we overvalue independence above this more humane interdependence. If we give our babies what they need to begin with, then they are perhaps more likely to move quickly to the next stage of being more independent and confident; but if we don't devote ourselves to them in the beginning, for fear of spoiling them or for fear of losing ourselves, our sleep, or our control, then maybe we will always have disengaged, demanding, or clingy children, who have either switched off or who are unconsciously complaining about unmet needs. Also, if we give our babies what they need to begin with, we may find we delight in them more and treasure each stage as special. I love my sleep, but if I have to be awake at 4 AM, then nothing beats breastfeeding my baby in the dark, just him and me together. I have found it both the toughest of times and also a very tender time. Many of today's parenting books, it seems to me, try to desensitize or shelter new mothers from those natural tensions and extremes and I wonder if the result doesn't often interfere with the natural bonding process and with our own development as mothers. Liedloff writes in *The Continuum Concept*:

> Custom has left the treatment of infants to maternal discretion. But should every mother be free to neglect her child, to slap him for crying, to feed him when she wants, not when he wants, to leave him suffering alone in a room for hours, days, months, when it is his very nature to be in the midst of life? The societies for the prevention of cruelty to babies and children concern themselves only with the grossest sort of abuse. Our society must be helped to see the gravity of the crime against infants that is today considered normal treatment.

Because I am aware that some attachment-parenting techniques have worked best in my family (such as breastfeeding, co-sleeping, wearing the baby in a sling, and responding quickly to his cues), and because I enjoy a healthy debate, I discussed this chapter with a psychologist friend who had found that many of the routine-based ideas recommended by writers such as Gina Ford were helpful in her family when her children were babies. I would not like to think there is only one right way of raising children. We all find ourselves inspired in different ways by different parenting books and Web sites, if we read them at all. She said:

> I have many friends who feel they parent according to different theoretical traditions, yet they all in reality parent very similarly, as part of a Western liberal tradition in which children are seen and heard and cherished...
>
> My reservations are that this position of attachment versus routine is rather artificial...
>
> It just doesn't represent what people actually do...Who are these routine parents who leave their baby to cry all night without comfort? Who are these attachment parents who never let their baby cry for a millisecond? I don't know any

of either. I also don't know anyone who consistently parents every minute of the day in the same way—on any one day I might respond in a myriad of ways from both and none of the childcare traditions. Don't others do the same? (Or do they, as I suspect, often feel guilt—the "routine" mom for just following the patterns of the child and not the schedule, and the "attachment" mom for feeling the relief of putting their child down or moving just that little more slowly toward their crying child?) This, to me, is the real problem with both such theoretical perspectives—they do not allow for dissent.

By picking up this book you have already revealed and started to explore your reflective and discerning (possibly dissenting?) nature. If you trust your instincts and trust your baby, you won't go far wrong. Jean Liedloff first wrote her book in the 1970s, at a time when many mothers were encouraged, often against their better judgment, to follow strict feeding schedules and to let their babies cry it out. Similar ideas are currently in fashion, but hopefully most people today do pick and choose their parenting styles, without being inconsistent, in order to best respond to their child's cues and their own needs on any one day. As one mother I interviewed says, "I have learn[ed] that I know my boy best and my instincts are most often right."

There is another point to be highlighted, and it is there in the thoughts of the psychologist friend above and in mine, despite our different preference in terms of general approach, and that is the importance of asking questions when we read or are given advice, questions based on our own knowledge of our own children and on our unique relationship with them. Slavishly adopting any one rule and applying it rigidly, simply because it is fashionable or touted by an expert (and who can be more expert than a child's own mother?), can be extremely unhelpful in the end. All children are unique, created individuals. We need to respond to them as special and unique creations of God in terms of their own personal needs and preferences, and our relationship with them. What works for one baby may not work for another—it depends on their temperament and also on the temperament of the parents. So, it is important to ask questions and to know our own children, otherwise, we can run into problems. One child psychologist I spoke to while researching this book commented that many of the families he saw professionally had some work to do in rebuilding the trust between parent and child after controlled crying or crying-it-out techniques had been rigidly and inappropriately applied. I have heard parents say, "We had to do controlled crying—you need strong nerves but it does work!," and "In the end we just had to let her cry it out," as if they had no choice when, in fact, there are important questions to be asked: "Why?", "How does it work?", "What might be the longer-term effects?", and "What are the alternatives for our baby?" Similarly, slavishly following all the attachment-parenting advice to carry your baby continuously, to co-sleep, and to breastfeed long term, might well be too exhausting for women to follow all the time if they have no help or have to be back at work quickly. Maternal burnout helps no one and what works in traditional cultures may not always be feasible in our own. And I know the crying issue is an emotive one. I found Deborah Jackson's book *When Your Baby Cries* helpful (see Further Reading). Use your discernment, and regard advice as an option to reflect on, not a rule, wherever it comes from. As one mother observes:

> It is about discerning the essence of a child, and I think that is an emotional and spiritual task which is quite difficult.
>
> *Hannah, mother of an 8-month-old daughter and*
> *a 2½-year-old daughter*

Another mother suggests:

> Take all the pieces of advice that are offered to you and choose which are going to suit you and your family. There are no right or wrong answers, just opinions. Don't have fixed ideas on the way things should be done, be willing to try alternatives.
>
> *Helen, mother of a 2-year-old son*

Trust your intuition, and your baby. We are often not used to tuning in to our intuitions, because our society generally values the outer and rational rather than the inner and instinctive. In some ways, we have become too civilized and in doing so have lost sight of our internal primal eye. The reflective exercises in this book are designed to help you to refind some of your natural instincts by tuning in to your inner life and instinctive feelings. I would suggest that it is here that the spiritual is experienced, too. Some of the ideas in chapter 1 might help you to do this as you try to discern what your baby's needs are, particularly the Examen prayer. Do you find a parenting strategy lifegiving or draining? Are you and your baby colorful or gray afterward?

Jean Liedloff, in *The Continuum Concept*, concludes:

> Once we fully realize the consequences of our treatment of babies, children, one another and ourselves, and learn to respect the real character of our species, we cannot fail to discover a great deal more of our potential for joy.

I wanted to approach parenting with imagination rather than a set of rules, and to develop fulfilling relationships with my children, not to regard them as adversaries to be controlled. I expect most parents share this. Discovering "our potential for joy" sounds like fun to me. You might find it a good yardstick as you search your own inspiring books and Web sites, and as you befriend your intuitions and instincts, to support you through your own unique experience.

Discovering Our Potential for Joy

Once your baby is born, he or she can be your greatest source of inspiration and joy—the tiny person who changes your life so dramatically is also the wonderful reason you can find the strength you need. This amazing baby is something you have made, yet original and new. Keeping a sense of wonder will help you to find inner reserves when you are tired or frustrated. When Thomas was born, we received so many cards, but one in particular sticks in my mind. Some contained humorous messages like "Now the real work begins!" and "It does get easier—after the first 18 years!", but my aunt sent a card in which she wrote, "Congratulations on the birth of your WONDERFUL new baby." She's right—new babies *are* wonderful. Try writing a list of the most wonderful things about your baby and your time together. Mine with my 5-month-old were:

- Stroking the soft skin on the back of your neck
- Kissing your tummy
- Stroking your nose
- Gazing into your ocean-deep blue eyes
- Spontaneously laughing together
- Feeling your little hand stroke my skin when I breastfeed
- Tickling your toes
- Playing "splash!" in the bath
- Smelling your downy head
- Watching you explore—your concentrated gaze
- Touching your soft, rosy cheeks
- Watching you try new tastes
- Holding your tiny hand
- Cradling your head when you fall asleep on my knee
- Chattering as you learn new sounds
- Watching your beautiful face

Then choose one thing a day to celebrate and enjoy—whisper in your baby's ear as you do, regardless of what else happens that day.

Many of the pleasures listed above are sensory pleasures. Jean Liedloff suggests that when babies are routinely deprived of touch and regular in-arms experience, their deprivation may in later life be expressed through illness, depression, or addictions. Only through feelings experienced under the influence of illicit substances, or through the attention the sick patient finally begins to receive from others, is their unspoken need for nurture and a feeling of well-being satisfied.

This reminded me of Jesus' healing ministry. Some New Testament theologians have suggested that there could have been a psychological component to these healings. Lepers, bleeding women, and so on were outcasts from normal society and considered ritually unclean. No one would want to touch them. The reason the priest and the Levite do not stop to help the man by the side of the road is that if he had been found to be dead, they would not have been able to fulfill their temple duties after touching him. But Jesus, in praising the actions of the Samaritan, is saying that our social duties to those in need take precedence over religious obligations. In touching the hemorrhaging woman and the lepers, he cuts through expected modes of behavior to help these people feel finally accepted, welcomed, and loved.

So, there is no doubt that touch is central to our sense of our own worth and well-being. This is important to remember in pregnancy. Even if you or your partner is not feeling very sexy, touch is still vital. It can be an affectionate part of your daily relationships with others. It is also important to remember the importance of touch for a newborn and for all our children. Maternity wards are realizing the importance of "skin-on-skin" contact between parents and their babies, and Jean Liedloff recommends constant 24-hour physical contact for new babies as the cornerstone to their feelings of being welcome and worthy as they grow up. This is a more extreme view, and not one that is very practical given the lack of extended family and community supporting most Western mothers, but her ideas nevertheless underline the pleasure and importance of nuzzling, cuddling, and holding our babies as much as we can, and of carrying them while we go about our daily lives so that they can observe and experience what they will soon be part of, and discover their environment while securely attached to an adult. Children start to learn how to respond to the world and to others from your example, while they are babies and in your close company, as you go out and about. This is not spoiling a baby; it is teaching a baby to love and to live. Older babies then start to move outward to explore their natural environment (your house), returning every now and then for the reassurance of physical contact—a hug—before continuing, and they like to "play" with the things they see mom and dad "playing" with, to feel they are joining in rather than being occupied elsewhere with irrelevant objects, hence their delight in remote controls for the TV, cell phones, spoons, boxes, makeup bags, keyrings, laptops, and so on. It beats filling your house with noisy jazzy plastic, if you have an aversion to it! Playpens, nurseries, and baby bassinets have their place, but are no substitute for the important developmental period of being in close and regular physical contact with a parent or other significant adult.

Of course, we can best welcome and involve our children and help them to feel innately worthy if we feel that way about ourselves. This may come more easily for some people than for others. Give yourself some space to discover your own potential for joy, so that, later, you can help your children discover theirs.

To this end, it may be helpful to think about what you need now, during your pregnancy and then in the busy weeks after the baby is born. What would be the most helpful advice the wisest mentor could give you? You may like to record the following guided visualization on tape to try, or ask a trusted friend or adviser to go through it with you.

Sit or lie quietly, and relax. Maybe play some peaceful music, light a candle, or burn some fragranced oil. Focus on your breathing—slow, measured, and deep...

Imagine yourself walking through a forest on a spring day, the sunlight dappling through the trees makes the day warm and the scent of the pine trees lingers in the air...The ground is soft and springy, carpeted with leaves and wild flowers, blue and yellow...You stop to touch a tree, to feel its bark and to notice its age and strength...You wind your way down a narrow path, between the ferns and saplings, deeper and deeper into the forest...It is an ancient and calming place to be, and you are feeling calm, because you are here with a purpose...In the heart of the forest there is a clearing where a freshwater spring bubbles up and over the rocks, forming a stream...You cup your hand into the water and take a drink ...At the head of the spring there is a figure, seated on the ground. This is the wisest person in the world...She motions to you to join her. She is inviting you to sit beside her, and she is welcoming, reassuring...You know now that you can ask her a question, but only one...While you are calm and enjoying the presence of the wisest person, consider your question and choose your time to ask it...When you have heard all you need to hear, thank the wisest woman and leave, keeping her response in your heart.

It might be helpful to find yourself an inspiring pregnancy mentor such as a more experienced friend or relative whom you respect or someone suggested to you by others—your church might be able to put you in touch with a spiritual director or someone trained to accompany others on their faith journey. It would certainly be a good idea to discern what you need in order to feel good—to feel relaxed, supported, and nurtured—while pregnant, and to try to put this in place so that you can continue after your baby is born. Looking after yourself so that you can look after your baby is important; it is a time to be concerned with your own desires and needs above other duties and obligations. It is a time to listen to your still inner voice and become your own inspirational mentor.

During my first pregnancy the Web site <http://www.storknet.com> featured an article by Jennifer Louden called "Nurturing Yourself During Pregnancy." In it the author advises: "The kernel, the gist, the essence of nurturing yourself during pregnancy is treating yourself like you are in the womb. Learning to believe you have the right to be cared for by others, to be supported." She comments further: "While it should be obvious that taking good care of the fetus growing inside of you is crucial, pregnancy isn't solely about the baby. It is also about you...." I found a new confidence while I was expecting: I was much more certain about standing up for the baby than I had ever been about standing up for myself. It can be helpful to pause to consider, would I stand for this for my baby? Is it good enough for him or her? If the answer is "No," then it's "No" for you too. Pregnancy can be a time of greater resolve and, therefore, a good time to address family, social, or professional situations that are not suiting you. My sister says, "It has made me worry less about what others think and think more about what's really important." Another mom says, "It has made me relax about a lot of things. Things that seemed highly important a few months ago now seem utterly irrelevant!" And a different mom, "I worry less... Having a baby has taught me to slow down. I don't rush around so much. Tom is my main priority." Knowing what you would ideally like, and having a greater motivation to negotiate toward it, can be empowering. Clarifying your desires and asking for what you need can enhance your sense of self, a sense which, during pregnancy, can feel uncertain. Jennifer Louden advises writing a list of things you need. I suggest completing the following sentence ten times, and regularly:

To enjoy my pregnancy today I desire...

Include the seemingly trivial (a foot massage, nice maternity clothes, chocolate) and the seemingly important (financial security, time with a friend, a new furnace, a shorter or longer break from work). Use your lists as a starting point for discerning, through time, prayer, and reflection, true desires from transient wishes. This process of discernment might be triggered by circling the things on your list you could manage without if you had to, and underlining what really does feel essential to your well-being. After that, don't rush it, but keep your list around and review it. It may be that what turns out to be really important for your well-being can be summarized in a few concepts (for example, rest, comfort, shared responsibility and preparation, understanding). Jennifer Louden writes:

> When you are feeling conflicted or unable to relax, talk with the voice of your pregnancy...Pregnancy provides a unique inner voice, what I think of as the energy of life, which can calm you and remind you what is important.

Learn to listen to and to use this voice. This could be one key to achieving a happy and centered, enjoyable pregnancy, and the strategy will continue to serve you well as you start a new kind of life with your baby.

Images of God

As Christians, we can find support and inspiration in our faith, particularly through prayer. In the gospels, when Jesus wants to pray he goes off by himself to find a quiet place (see, for example, Luke 4:42; 6:12). More often than not, people follow him and he ends up meeting their needs and sacrificing his own quiet time. This is a bit like parenthood. It can be hard to find a few minutes for ourselves and a quiet place away from a baby, but we do all need time out to recover some energy and to take stock, and this time can include prayer time.

Try simply imagining your ideal place to pray. The beauty of this is that your prayer place can be anywhere you like because you are visiting it with your mind's eye rather than physically. Is it by a lake, in a forest, or on top of a mountain? It might be in a building or room of some kind. Imagine somewhere that is your special place, and which is quiet so that you can meet God there. Find a way of quieting down inside, and imagine yourself in this place, each time you prepare to pray or to spend some quiet time. You could try this while you are feeding your baby, or relaxing in the bath if you are pregnant, or even while you are cooking or walking or falling asleep at night. For a while, my place was a beach at sunset, with a large bed on it, lots of white billowing sheets, pillows, and duvets and absolutely no one else. This image was my prayerful "getting back to sleep after being woken up" place for quite some time!

Once you've got the hang of this and have visited your prayer place a few times, it will start to feel familiar to you. Then you can see if you can notice your surroundings in more detail. How do you get there? Are you walking, standing, or sitting? How do you leave? How does God meet you here? In this story from 1 Kings 19:9–13, the prophet Elijah meets God in a special and maybe surprising way:

> [Elijah] traveled forty days and forty nights until he reached Horeb, the mountain of God. There he went into a cave and spent the night.
>
> And the word of the LORD came to him: "What are you doing here, Elijah?"
>
> …The LORD said, "Go out and stand on the mountain in the presence of the LORD, for the LORD is about to pass by."
>
> Then a great and powerful wind tore the mountains apart and shattered the rocks before the LORD, but the LORD was not in the wind. After the wind there was an earthquake, but the LORD was not in the earthquake. After the earthquake came a fire, but the LORD was not in the fire. And after the fire came a gentle whisper. When Elijah heard it, he pulled his cloak over his face and went out and stood at the mouth of the cave (NIV).

Does being in your imaginary place help you to notice the gentle breeze of God's spirit when it passes by? What inspires and speaks to you?

This story is surprising because we might expect God to be in the powerful wind, earthquake, and fire, but he isn't. He is gentle and quiet and might not have been noticed if Elijah hadn't been listening.

Father	Light	Teacher
Shepherd	Lord	Miracle-maker
King	Wisdom	Transcendent
Servant	Ever-present	Immanent
Judge	All-seeing	Dwelling in everyone
Advocate	All-powerful	Dwelling in nature
Comforter	All-knowing	
Creator	Bringing justice	Merciful
Forgiving	Bringing freedom	Compassionate
Loving unconditionally	Concerned for the poor and those on the margins	Infinite
Personal		Mother
Friend	Healer	
	Master	

Elijah is very open-minded about what God might be like. Maybe we rely on just one or two images of what God is like —perhaps we need to let ourselves imagine God in different ways. The authors (Dennis Linn et al.) of a book called *Good Goats —Healing Our Image of God* make the point that we become like the God we adore. So, if we want to be compassionate, accepting, and patient, it is no good imagining God to be like, in their words, "Good old Uncle George…bearded, gruff and threatening." Projecting onto God all your own parents' worst faults doesn't help either, and very often there is an image of our own parents or parent at the heart of our image of God. This can, of course, be a helpful thing if our parents were nurturing, and it's worth remembering how we might come across to our own children. We are patterns to them, and we will inspire them—what will they learn about God from us? In the New Testament the Holy Spirit is described as an advocate, that is, like someone who is on your side, seeking justice, speaking convincingly for you, supporting you, and wanting you to be free. *Good Goats* quotes Meister Eckhart: "The seed of God is in us...Pear seeds grow into pear trees, nut seeds into nut trees, and God seed into God." If, after thinking about this, you feel your image of God is unhelpful and limits you, try exploring some others. In the box on page 92 is a list of phrases and images that might be used by Christians about God. You could copy it and checkmark the ones that appeal to you and cross out the ones that don't. Then spend some time thinking about your preferences, how far they can be helpful and inspiring to you, and which you would like your child to see in you.

Our images of God depend on our experiences of God. This struck me some years ago when, for a period, I felt let down by God. When I asked myself what sort of God I felt had let me down, I realized that I was thinking of the God I had heard about, read about, thought I prayed to, and thought I believed in—it was actually quite a traditional set of images. I decided to think back over my spiritual life to try to identify what my own personal experience of God honestly was—with surprising results. I realized that, for me, God is powerful, creative, beautiful and illuminating, life-giving, and on my side. These continue to be helpful images for me, rather than "all-powerful," "judge," or "teacher," although these may be very helpful images for others.

Two experiences in particular helped me to understand and know God in my own way. First, as a teenager I was interested in charismatic worship. At a group meeting one evening, as someone spoke in tongues, I had what I can only describe as a vision of a red tulip unfolding to reveal the yellow and black center before becoming a butterfly and fluttering up and away. It was a vibrantly colorful, powerful, and alive picture, and the beauty of it took my breath away. I knew I hadn't generated it myself. When the tongues were interpreted, the speaker described exactly what I had just seen, the flower being God's love for me unfolding and taking wing. Red tulips still remind me of God every spring. The screensaver on my computer is a slideshow of family photos, but I've included in the series a photo of a red tulip, so that when it suddenly appears on the screen I am reminded to stop for a few seconds to enjoy the present moment.

Second, at a time when I was reluctantly changing jobs and moving away from a much-loved area, a mental picture (not a vision, this time!) kept recurring to me, and it was of an angel standing behind me pointing forward, as if to say, "Go!" It was a picture I could call to mind whenever I needed to. This angel was no cherub or white-robed painting, but a huge, dark, granite, strong angel. This image stayed with me after I had made the move, but changed slightly over the months as I took some time to recover from what had been an emotionally difficult period: it still stood behind me, but its wings closed firmly around me, protective. As a few years passed the image returned as I knew that, while I was happy enough, I did not want my circumstances to stay the same forever. This time the angel was billowing out behind me, as if stirring up a wind, and the words that went with it were, "gathering momentum." Shortly afterward, I met Stephen and life changed dramatically and brought me to the more fulfilled place I am in today. I now live in the Northeast, and regularly drive past Antony Gormley's sculpture *The Angel of the North*. The statue is made of rusty steel and is shaped like a jumbo jet. It is the largest public sculpture in Europe—massive. It is a symbol of regeneration, hope, and strength, and it reminds me of my own angel, which I believe was from God. It isn't an image I use so much now, but I did have a sense of its presence, standing just to one side, watching over me, when I had my cesarean section.

So, as you think about your own images of God, try to decide which are there because that is what you have been taught, and which are there because that is what you have experienced. There may be some very surprising, but very legitimate, differences.

In *The Continuum Concept*, Jean Liedloff writes about the feeling of serenity that so many of us seek. She suggests that as a species and as babies we experienced this feeling, and lost it as we began, collectively and individually, to be able to think and to make choices. Many of the ways in which we try to regain this serenity, such as making love, drinking alcohol, yoga, exercise, massage, and so on, are actually ways of turning off the thinking process. She has an interesting take on the role of meditation—and perhaps, by implication, of contemplative prayer:

> *Meditation* is the word usually given to this procedure of dethinking. It is at the center of many schools of discipline that seek to raise the serenity level. A commonly used technique is the repetition of a mantra, a word or phrase, as an eraser of thoughts of the associative kind that the mind tends to pursue. As the procession of thoughts is slowed and stopped, the physiological state of the subject changes to resemble, in certain ways, that of an infant. Breathing becomes shallower, and recent experiments have shown that brain waves are produced of a sort that are unlike those of either adult wakefulness or adult sleep. For those who meditate regularly, there is an apparent increase in serenity, sometimes called spirituality, which lends a stabilizing influence to the rest of their time.

She goes on to quote ritual as another device that allows the intellect to rest so that we can begin to recapture the feelings of serenity we should have had—and can certainly provide for our own children—as babies held in arms for a good deal of time. It interested me to note that she does not refer to an external God; spirituality for her seems to be about regaining a positive infant experience, not a transcendent adult one, but you can decide for yourself if her description of the experience of prayer and worship rings true for you.

We have looked in chapter 2 at different ways of praying, and on pages 90 and 91 at where we pray and how prayer helps us feel. The Bible quotes below can certainly be used as a prayer aid, but I have included them here because they are quotes that I find inspire, comfort, and calm me. They are helpful for me to keep written on a card in my bag, or by the bed, when I'm stressed or going through a time of change:

- "Guard me as the apple of the eye; / hide me in the shadow of your wings" (Psalm 17:8).
- "Be still, and know that I am God!" (Psalm 46:10).
- "If I take the wings of the morning / and settle at the farthest

limits of the sea, / even there your hand shall lead me, / and your right hand shall hold me fast" (Psalm 139:9–10).

- "This is what the Lord asks of you: only this, to act justly, to love tenderly and to walk humbly with your God" (Micah 6:8).
- "...My peace I give to you...do not let your hearts be troubled, and do not let them be afraid" (John 14:27).
- "Let us love one another; because love is from God; and everyone who loves is born of God and knows God" (1 John 4:7).

I also have two cards from the Carmelite Monastery in Norfolk, with beautiful photographs on one side and inspiring quotes on the other:

- "One does not discover new lands without first consenting to lose sight of the shore" (André Gide).
- "Life is only for love, time is only that we may find God" (Saint Bernard).

Finding inspirational quotes—from Scripture, from famous people, from poems, from self-help books—and writing them down, attaching them to your mirror, or putting them in your car, is a good way of reminding yourself about God and about what really matters to you as you go about your daily life. When we have babies we may only have time for mini-prayers of this kind, and that's fine.

Here are some other activities that may help you to discover a source of inner inspiration and calm. They are designed to be more challenging, but they can also be fun and could help you to see yourself positively and more clearly:

- What shape is your mood? If you could draw it as a cartoon character, what would the caption be?
- Think of three adjectives that describe you. Take each one in turn and try spending a day being the opposite, just to see how it feels. You may hate it, or you may find it refreshing—in either case, it's a good way of helping us to identify some of the patterns we adopt. We can then think about changing them if we want to, or investing in them if they are helpful.
- What are you most thankful for, and how do you show it? How

would you most like your family and friends to show their thanks to you?

- What would you like people to say about you? How would this make you feel? Take a few moments to think about your best qualities and how you display them.

- Imagine turning your TV off for one week. What could you do instead of watching it? Give it a go. Remove it from the room completely and think about what else could be the room's focal point for a few days—maybe the fireplace, or a vase of flowers, a group of house plants, or a display of some kind. How does this change the atmosphere in the room? Research shows people feel happier if they watch less TV, partly because they are then less exposed to images of a lifestyle they don't have and possessions they don't own but might like, and partly because they use the time to invest in other things—people, for instance, or pets. So, if you like animals, how about ditching the TV in favor of a kitten? Far more entertaining! (But not very practical with a new baby, perhaps—you can't put a diaper on a kitten.) More seriously, Sally Ward in her book *Baby Talk* makes the point that babies cannot differentiate very well between background and foreground noise. If the TV is always on, your baby will have a harder time picking out your voice when you talk. This is a shame in terms of your relationship, and it can also affect the baby's development because TV discourages the social inter-action that babies need in order to learn and thrive. So, learning to live quietly at times has big benefits.

- Think about the most important people in your life. Jot down a list of the things you like best about them, and then let them know. A good time to try this with your partner is Valentine's Day, over dinner. Try it with older children on their birthdays —write your list inside their card. Make this a family tradition and ask people to do it for you too.

Making the decision to have a child is momentous. It is to decide forever to have your heart go walking around the outside of your body.

Elizabeth Stone, author

5

New Parental Roles and Adapting to Family Life

There are two lasting bequests we can give our children: one is roots, the other is wings.

Hodding Carter, journalist and Pulitzer Prize winner

"Chicken-Banana" Days

Before we had a child, Stephen and I would go to the movies, to concerts, and wine bars more often, leave household tasks and shopping until later, eat out, and generally enjoy the young, free life we had. I knew it was Friday because we would be tired from the workweek, there would be clothes all over the bedroom, and no food in the house. We used to call these times "chicken-banana"days—there would be a blackened banana in the fruit bowl and a lump of frozen chicken somewhere at the back of the freezer, and that was it. We would joke about what we could make (chicken, flavored with essence of banana; banana infused with the delicate aroma of grated chicken; banana stuffed with…er…banana). Then, we'd call for takeout or pick a nice restaurant.

It is important to avoid those chicken-banana days once babies come along. Preserve your reserves. You need to look after yourself, so that you can look after your baby. And this means making your surroundings comfortable and ensuring there are nice things to eat and drink in your cupboards.

This is not intended to sound superficial. In all likelihood, you will be spending more time in your house than ever before, which can feel strange when you're used to working, so think in advance about what will make it conducive to peace and pleasure. The lifestyle changes and financial changes that come with pregnancy and birth can seem hard, and cooking at home can help here too—it's cheaper, and can be both fun and valuable time together with your partner. Household mess and clutter have never helped me to feel relaxed, despite the advice of a multitude of baby books to lower domestic standards at this time. I hasten to add, we don't live in a show house, but we do notice the difference a cared-for and nurturing home environment makes. If you need a tasteful toy box in each room to make tidying easier, nutritious and tempting food in the 'fridge, some help with the ironing, and a clean bathroom with lovely toiletries in it, then do what you can to plan ahead for those so that they are there when you feel you might soon reach the end of your rope. If your favorite comfort food is toast and peanut butter and marshmallow creme, stock up with it.

In other words, make your home a nice place to be in, not just to pass through. I mean this literally, but also symbolically: find an inner peace and sense of self-worth so that *you* are a nice place to be, too. Some of the earlier ideas for prayer in this book may help you to do this internally and on a spiritual level.

Preserving your reserves is important emotionally and spiritually when you are a 4 AM madonna.

This is especially noteworthy if you are raising children by yourself. It's also a big issue if, like me and many new mothers today, you live a long way from the traditional support networks of extended family and old friends. There is an African proverb, "It takes a village to raise a child." Historically, raising babies has been a community affair and we are perhaps the first generation of women facing the phenomenon of being by ourselves with small children for much of the time. Often new grandparents, even if they do live close by, are healthy enough and well-heeled enough to be enjoying an active retirement, and may not want to be as available as their own parents or grandparents might have been. New aunts often work, so there is less of a network of women at home. One mother said to me:

> I think having children is hard enough, but our society, disparate and divided up, makes us go into this situation with no experience and no clue of what to do—consequently I felt completely at sea in the early days in every sense, as a person, as a wife, and as a mother, I didn't know how to do anything.

Now I have much more confidence in my own mothering, but still find it endlessly challenging as my children hit new stages …The isolation can be tremendous.

Jean Liedloff writes: "A woman left alone every day with her children is deprived of social stimulation and needs emotional and intellectual support which they cannot give. The result is bad for mother, child, family and society." Clarissa Pinkola Estés suggests that we have lost the art of caring for our mothers, leaving them to "self-mother." She writes that, ideally, "a mother must be mothered in mothering her own offspring." However, this is no longer what happens: "In most parts of industrialized countries today, the young mother broods, births, and attempts to benefit her offspring all by herself. It is a tragedy of enormous proportions." We can learn from other cultures here. In Sikhism, mothers are revered because a mother is regarded as a new baby's first religious and spiritual teacher. Traditionally, a Sikh mother does not leave the house for 40 days after the birth; postpartum appointments are held in her home, and she is attended to by the female members of her extended family, who take over the running of the house for this period so that she can rest.

Our own society is diminished by its lack of support for mothers. I am amazed at how many facilities for disabled people I need to use with a stroller—from ramps to toilets to automatic doors and elevators. Very rarely do these facilities carry a parent and child symbol next to the picture of a wheelchair, and yet proportionately there must be more parents with strollers than wheelchair users who are in need of facilities that help them to access mainstream life. The importance of mothering, of having your baby with you most of the time so that you can create that internal space for this new person, of being able to hold your baby, feed your baby, is not recognized— mothers must leave their babies somewhere else, or stay out of mainstream life themselves. Any of your own appointments—hair, dentist, well-woman checkups, and banking—have to be done in baby-free time. Which is when, exactly? Is it 11 AM on a Saturday, vying for that one appointment along with every other mother? Or, do you take your baby with you and put up with the inconvenience and ignore the disapproval? What do you do if you want to take a class or go on a retreat, or have a facial, or go to see a film or museum or art exhibition? There is little reason why children should not be welcome, yet often they are not once they are past the newborn sleepy stage, and so most women are lucky if they can follow other interests and aspirations when they have small children. This surely has some kind of impact on the statistics for postpartum depression in the Western world. No wonder so many new mothers discover a subculture of coffee mornings, toddler groups, and so on—it is because there is a huge set of people out there who are effectively barred from normal culture, normal activities, and often from any other aspirations they may have.

This has a longer-term effect: the fact that many mothers are isolated, and space is not generally made in society for babies, means that both girls and boys are growing up without seeing examples all around them of mothering and of babies. There are restricted examples around for them to observe and, later, to copy. It is not normalized. Motherhood is a big enough transition, but maybe it would be easier if it had a more open and welcomed public place.

You are bigger than your baby and have more facets to your personality than simply mothering, but your baby and mothering will demand a lot of you in today's world. If at first you have a "Velcro baby" who cries a lot and won't be put down, as I did, then the demands are greater. After six months at home with my new baby, and having resigned from my job with an organization that didn't offer part-time flexible working or family-friendly hours (for me, working part-time might have provided a healthy balance), we used daycare for one afternoon a week. Mainly, this was writing time for me, but partly it was also, in all honesty, simply time to be everything else that I am. If I had lived a few generations earlier, and stayed near my hometown and extended family, I may not have needed to do this. In the end, one afternoon with good daycare gave our baby the opportunity to play with older children and relate to other adults in a family setting, which he enjoyed, and it gave me some time, space, and an intellectual outlet. The arrangement cost no more than the price of a takeout meal. I'd sacrifice the takeout any time if it meant I could find that inner peace and outward calm. Whatever your social and financial situation, it's up to you to find a balance between being there and giving yourself for your baby, and making sure you have what you need both in your physical environment and inside yourself.

It is very easy to run out or reach rock bottom. As one mother in my circle wryly observes: "I do have 'going to the airport and never coming back' fantasies, and talking with friends, I don't think I'm the only one!" So again, consider in advance what you will need when those chicken-banana days loom. It could be one key to really enjoying your new baby.

Such days threaten to loom because you are going through great changes and developing fast, using lots of inner reserves. You have probably seen films of the cell division that occurs when the female ovum is fertilized. A single cell becomes two, then four, then eight, and all these changes take place very rapidly. I think it's a miraculous image. I also think this is an image that can represent the wider female psyche. Each role we develop in our lives becomes another dimension of us. Try the exercise below, and hopefully you'll see what I mean.

Draw a circle, which represents you. Think of a role you have —maybe you are someone's sister. Draw a line through the circle to represent that role. This is like that ovum dividing, or developing. You are a daughter, too, so draw another line. If you are someone's friend, if you have a job, a partner, and so on, draw more lines through your circle. Think widely about all the possible roles you have developed so far in your life. What you will end up with is a circle with many facets—one single person who has developed in so many different ways, and adapted herself in so many different roles. Now that you are becoming a mother, you will have a very big line to draw through that circle. This exercise is not intended to suggest a splitting of your personality, but a developing of it that helps you grow each time: multiplication, not division. Think of each line as a turn of a kaleidoscope.

The Shape of Things to Come...

In this section, we'll be looking at how our sense of self, family, and relationships change when a baby comes along, so that we can assimilate those changes more readily. While this is an inner process, it can have an impact on our physical space too.

Having a baby changes the shape of the relationship you have with your partner. When there are just the two of you, your relationship is linear: imagine a line between two people, along which communication, love, physical affection, experience, support, understanding, spatial accommodation, and so on pass back and forth.

Rachel  Stephen

Now imagine what happens when this becomes a three-way relationship.

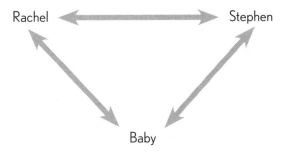

Rachel   Stephen

Baby

In her book *What Mothers Do, Especially When It Looks Like Nothing* (see Further Reading), psychotherapist and mother Naomi Stadlen writes:

> Some people have compared the baby to a "wedge" driving the couple apart. But it's easy to blame the baby. True, the couple relationship feels different. However, there may be a different way to explain it. What few parents mention is the momentous change that comes about when a two-person couple relationship suddenly opens out into a three-person one... A two-person relationship is radically different from one of

three people. A two-person relationship has a kind of elegant symmetry, whereas this three-person one is complex.

For this new triangular relationship to be successful, the communication, love, physical affection, experience, support, understanding, spatial accommodation, and so on must travel along all three lines, not just along the original line between the mother and father or, as sometimes happens, just along the new line between the mother and baby. Sometimes, when this does happen, it can be because the father sees it as her baby and opts out of the triangle, or it can be because the mother becomes so consumed by her new relationship with the baby that it takes the place of her original, linear relationship. Either way, where the triangle is not recognized and honored and where a linear relationship (along any one line on the diagram) is dominant, people run into problems. The new mother and the new father both need to stay in relationship with each other, but each needs also to create an inner and external space for the new relationship with their baby. This will of course change the couple's own relationship because a new dimension is added to it that both need to accommodate.

A second baby turns the family relationship into a square shape, a third baby turns the shape into an octagon, and so on. Each additional baby's experience will be unique, as he or she is born into a family shape that is different from the one into which siblings were born. The challenge for the family is to adapt to, honor and make space for these changing shapes. This is a very complex thing to do, because each additional child rapidly multiplies the number of relationships forming within the family unit. Two adults have one relationship. A family with two adults and one child has three relationships. A family with two adults and two children has six relationships to accommodate, and another child makes for ten relationships:

A relationship between two adults looks like this:

Adult  Adult

The relationships in a one-child family look like this:

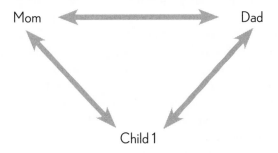

The relationships in a two-child family look like this:

And the relationships in a three-child family look like this:

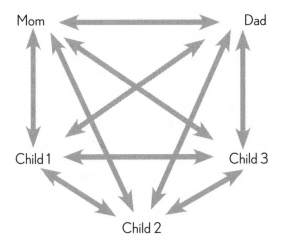

In addition, family counselors often talk about there being an invisible and equal but permeable line between the generations. The communication, love, physical affection, experience, support, understanding, spatial accommodation, and so on that is embodied in the family can travel through this line, between the generations. Each member of each generation is equal to all other members of the family in this respect, but this line does mean that they might appropriately be treated differently. So, in our diagram below, Thomas is equal to Rachel and Stephen in terms of the love each person feels and receives, in terms of the validity of their experiences, their need to communicate and be heard, their need for their own space, and their need for physical affection from each other.

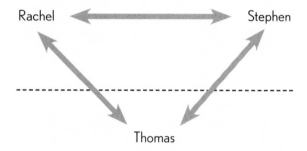

But the line also has implications—not for the shape of the family relationships, but for the way in which different generations in the family relate to each other, and the language they use. So Thomas will have some decisions made for him, like what he eats and what he wears, because he's a baby. If Rachel and Stephen made those sorts of decisions for each other without a discussion, there might be an argument. Thomas' dependency travels up the line to be met by his parents, and Stephen and Rachel's responsibility travels down the line to meet the needs of their child. Dependency and responsibility do not travel *across* to members of the same generation in quite the same way (obviously this is flexible; if your partner is ill, you may respond to his temporarily increased dependency on you as appropriate, but without assuming the role or behaving as if you were his mother). So this line is what requires a woman to treat her partner as an adult, not one of the children, and vice versa. It is what requires a father to be physical with his partner in a different way than he is physical with his children, even though physical affection is shown to all members of the family. If a parent is single, then different adaptations will be made to the home environment to welcome a new partner than those made on welcoming a new baby, even though all new members are welcomed and made space for. It is a line that can help to explain the relationship between grandparents and grandchildren, which can sometimes be very close but not take the place of a parental relationship. Different generations relate in different but equal ways in families that function well. A healthy relationship between a grandparent and grandchild is different than a healthy parent-child relationship, in terms of how they relate, the language they use, and the responsibilities that come with each role. The two relationships should not, ideally, be in conflict because they are different. A grandparent does not have the same responsibilities toward a child as its parents. But an elderly woman might still need to mother her adult daughter when that daughter has her own babies, as a way of meeting that daughter's needs at a specific point in her life. This line means you could, ideally, phone your mom and ask her to do some cooking for you when a new baby arrives, without that request giving her the right to comment critically on how you choose to bring up that baby. Relationships between different generations are at their best when they are mutually respectful and loving, but also recognizing of this invisible, equal, permeable line and the different roles, dependencies, and responsibilities it brings.

So, family members are equal but treated appropriately differently. This opens up all sorts of scenarios in which children might be included in family decision making, for instance. If everyone is equal, then everyone must be included in decision making, but in appropriately different ways. Problems may arise if adults have adult expectations of their children, but also if they regard their children as irrelevant in the family shape or relationship, and then exclude them from decision making.

Gender becomes important too (see diagram on page 108). Imagine an invisible band drawn around those family members who share the same gender: what effects might this have on family dynamics?

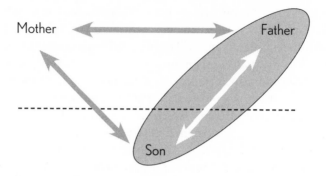

How far are any of these observations relevant in your family, and how far might you need to reflect on changes you'd like to see in your family's dynamics?

Having a baby brings changes in terms of roles, status, finance, and domestic arrangements within a family home and within a couple's relationship. It may be worth having a heartfelt and honest discussion with your partner about how each of you perceives these changes, and the value judgments you make about each one. Are your core values still being kept at the core? You could use the diagrams above as a starting point. I suggest *you* raise this issue, as having a baby still usually changes a woman's life much more than a man's, particularly if it also brings changes to her usual work arrangements.

If you go back to work full-time because you love your job or because your family relies on your income, remember that having a baby may well give you an emotional tug away from your work. This can be particularly stressful if you feel you have no option to do anything about it. Even if it's a positive choice, you may find your feelings compromised, just as you might if you give up work and miss the stimulus. These two moms found themselves adapting by adopting a more sustainable life-work balance:

> I was previously quite career minded; however, I am now more distanced from work. Consequently I find it easier to prioritize and I think I perform better while at work but can leave work behind and enjoy the time I have with Hannah.
>
> *Emma, eight months pregnant and mother of a 1-year-old daughter*

My work colleagues no longer have a totally career-focused person to work with and now every minute past the time when I should have been away from work is a minute less I get to spend with her.

Tracey, mother of an 8-month-old daughter

Each of these new moms managed to negotiate a four-day working week so that they could spend more time with their daughters.

For women cutting back on their working hours, or taking a career break, it is easy to fall into the trap of it being "his money"'and "her baby." If you get as far as "her washing machine," then it really is time for that chat! It might be helpful to look at the role of money in your lives. Is it what decides everything else? Are all decisions finance-based? Is earning money tacitly regarded as being of higher value than nurturing children or creating a home? Child care might be available and affordable and the professionals well qualified, but a parent's love and influence are irreplaceable. Some things have an emotional or spiritual value that cannot be "costed out" in a rational list. Much of what mothers do is unpaid and invisible, so women at home (and it's usually women, either on maternity leave or full time, but the same points apply to dads at home) can miss out on the status, sense of achievement (which includes knowing they are good at what they do), positive feedback, and value they may have enjoyed in the workplace. Is this really fair? Of course it isn't, but often it seems to be the case in an economy dominated by material productivity. But is playing with blocks really just playing with blocks, if you're playing with your own baby? How far is this lack of recognition happening to you and, if it is, then is it really an accurate reflection of your family's values? Might there be a basis for decision making that more clearly reflects your family's spiritual values and emotional needs?

I value intellectual stimulation—in fact, I require it to be happy, really. Using my mind, which God gave me, and honing it, is important to me. But I gave up a fulfilling job and career to look after my baby because having him fulfilled a very deep desire—I quickly felt infatuated with him and wanted to keep him near while he is young, and in the end I realized that I wanted to bring up my baby more than I wanted to work full-time, long hours and regularly away from home. But it was a tremendously difficult decision because I also realized that I would go bonkers very quickly if baby care shaped every day, with no intellectual or social outlets. This presented a dilemma—I'm not a trendy "glamor-girl" mom, and I don't bake cakes. One course of action for women in this situation is, of course, to support campaigns for greater flexibility within the work environment for the parents of preschool children, so that new parents' professional skills, expertise, and experience are not lost from the workplace if they decide to spend more time bringing up their children, and so that children benefit from being with their parents. We are still some way from this at the moment. My own solution was to start to write this book and to send a sample chapter off to publishers, employing a babysitter for a few hours a week once I got the go-ahead. I've also enrolled in a year's course for a day a week, which I could not have done while working, and which, with a bit of imagination and flexibility from myself and the course leaders (who are setting a ground-breaking example, I think), I will be able to take our next baby along to. This has by no means been an easy process, but I am lucky in that I have a supportive and encouraging husband who was prepared to work an extra evening clinic so that I could stop working for a while, and in order for our children to have the family life and home life to which we are both committed. Financially, there isn't much room for extras, and yes, by pay day we've usually slipped into the red. As we met in our thirties and enjoyed well-traveled, well-wined-and-dined twenties, we have had to adjust—but that's OK for now and we feel God is looking after us and that our choices were clearly discerned. All our finances are joint and we have a shared vision, which we each contribute to in very specific and very different ways, and we do it as a team. In the future, things may be different and we may each play different parts.

How will you honor your values and weave them into the fabric of your life, along with everything else that makes up that rich tapestry? Be creative! Go back to the drawing board and think outside the box if necessary. How are you going to make it all work for you and your family so that you are all (including your baby) fulfilled and happy? Many parents of either gender do what they need to do, but maybe, if you stop and think and let your feelings have a voice, you can find a way of doing what you *want* to do. This applies to dads too—children, whether babies or teenagers, need to see their fathers and spend time with them. It is important for their personal development and self-esteem that they have involved fathers as role models. Going back to earlier comments, this will be harder to do if earning money is the deciding factor regardless of other desires. If you both enjoy stimulating jobs that bring in the cash and hopefully buy nice things, *and* if both of you and your children are happy and fulfilled, with plenty of time together, then fine—carry on, because you have no problem. And I know that many people don't have much choice because money is tight or there is only one family income. But most people, when considering a change and what they need to live on, think above and beyond what they think they need to pay for. You'd be surprised at what you can do without if you decide to cut back—which may not sound like much fun, but neither is forty-five hours a week in daycare for lots of babies, perhaps. And many people find that, once they take the plunge, simple living can be very satisfying. Catherine Whitmire, author of *Plain Living* (see Further Reading), says of her own decision to be less work/money focused, "This simplification process was not about 'sacrifice' but about choosing the life I really wanted." She also quotes Parker J. Palmer, "Before you tell your life what you intend to do with it, listen for what it intends to do with you," and Christina Hadley Snyder, "Simplicity is not so much about what we own, but about what owns us. If we need lots of possessions to maintain our self-esteem and create our self-image...then we have forgotten or neglected that which is real and inward."

So, when you work out how you want to live "postbaby," use your discernment, rather than assuming you have no choice. There are some good books for people who are thinking about this sort of lifestyle change, and I've included some in the Further Reading section. It is unfortunate that having babies often coincides with career advances. It all seems to happen at the same point in life, and it is easy for either partner to overstretch themselves just when their families are young and in need of their parents. However, we can be audacious and put our time with our family first for a few years. What I am saying is that if you are all OK, great—but if it feels like it's not working for you, then it probably isn't, and you may be able to do something about it. Nothing is for ever, but you can't buy back a childhood.

As if lifestyle changes are not enough to contend with, adapting to new roles as mom and dad can, it seems, also raise unforeseen tensions in a healthy relationship that need to be recognized and talked through. Often a couple find themselves thrown into the traditional roles they thought they were too modern, too independent, or too educated to embrace. The parody in the box on p. 113 pulls together all the worst possible moments of the worst possible day everymother might feel she's gone through. Try to imagine this as a cartoon strip (with you and your beloved in the leading roles, if it's appropriate), and see if any bells ring true.

Of course, the situation portrayed in the box is a clichéd picture, but bits of it happen to many couples if only occasionally—many women might ruefully catch a glimmer of self-recognition in places. It's demoralizing for mom, trying for dad, and it's worth looking at what is really going on. If bits of this ring true in terms of your own emotional state, then talk it through and read on. If bits of it ring true because your partner really could be more engaged, then also talk it through and read on. It's easy to provide endless patience and endless fun when you are not actually having to do it endlessly. But when women at home are doing it all day (and, again, with a newborn it is usually mom on maternity leave, but the same points apply vice versa in families that reverse roles) and for most of the nighttime parenting time too, it can feel endless and it's impossible to perform all the time—particularly at a time when your self-identity is changing as quickly as your hormones. Looking after babies and small children is exhausting and challenging, but with understanding and support (emotional and practical) from others, it can be overridingly rewarding and fulfilling—and tremendously important for the child. New parents need to try to understand and support each other, and to recognize and accept such offers, in order that each might find those beautiful memories.

However much they love their baby, the parent at home might need to get out of the home, with or without the baby, to interact with other adults or to pursue different interests quite regularly, in order to avoid feeling like the woman in the parody on p. 113. As a couple, how can you arrange for this? By the end of the day (which

You are New Mom and it's LIFE, girl, but not as you know it! You've had a good day, particularly considering your days are still so unlike anything you have ever experienced before. You've nuzzled, kissed, nurtured, changed, and fed your newborn easily and happily in moments of bliss, gone out and about, napped a little...aahhh! But suddenly, it's 5 PM and you turn into a weird hysterical mad witch... desperate for no apparently sane reason to hand the baby over—especially if the baby is irritable—out of sight, out of earshot, out of the house if possible. New Dad arrives home when you are at your worst. You feel he never sees you any other way. You wonder if he is wondering why you haven't washed your hair? Vacuumed? You wonder if he's wondering why he's getting the brunt of it all and supporting you financially too? He listens patiently (patronizingly? you ask yourself; condescendingly?) and as you irrationally suspect he's also making judgments about how well you are coping with what might seem like quiet domesticity (easy? boring? unimportant?), he irritates you to death. He enjoys a fun half hour with the baby while you scramble together a meal. You think he's more fun than you. You think your baby prefers him. He says, "Do you need any help?" over his shoulder as he tickles Junior. He's particularly patient when the baby cries. The baby cries less with him. This makes you cry and you start to wonder how you've turned into this neurotic, paranoid, ungrateful drudge whom no one could possibly want to live with, or, who can't possibly share a house with any other living creature—depending on your temperament...He gets a better night's sleep than you and asks you in the morning, "Were you up much with the baby?" You want to smash a bedside lamp. Then he makes you some toast as you gaze at your beautiful and adorable newborn, before taking the baby for an hour while you lie in. You feel soft and tender and lovely again—and guilty as hell.

is 6 PM, not 10 PM), mom and baby are both ready for a break and a change of scene, as are working dads. However, a mother's quiet presence and changing modes are what the baby experiences while with her, and this is not to be subordinated or valued less than exciting time with dad. Quiet normality is more realistic over an entire day than constant frolicking and it is the cornerstone of a child's experience of home life, provided by fathers in households that reverse the traditional roles. Babies learn best about life when a parent is available and around for them to observe in a quiet, ordinary way. They do not thrive on constant speed and noise. So the parent who is at home needs to feel that what they do is valuable. Working dads often have the energy to be exciting because the chance to play with their baby is a welcome break in their corporate day. And often they don't have the energy and are exhausted after a day at work on limited sleep, but, like you, they make a special effort for their children and partner. Many new dads face feelings of financial responsibility to which they are unaccustomed, just as many new moms are facing new responsibilities at home and as the main caregivers for tiny new people, and playing giddy games when they get home can help them unwind. It's fun for the baby too—in our evolutionary past your baby would have been swinging through trees clinging onto one of you! And sometimes, because of the novelty and because they may not be as uninhibited with someone they spend less time with, babies do cry less. It is not something for the parent at home to resent because the working parent needs to feel appreciated too, and needs time to get to know their babies in their own way.

Babies do not need two moms. They may optimally need two parents. Moms and dads can offer different things. My advice to couples is not to try to compete with each other, but to recognize each other's gifts. Different people offer different things, but both are equal and actually make up a complete picture. The important thing is to communicate rather than compete, share instead of snap, and to try to understand and value each other's experiences as new parents. For more on this subject, Naomi Stadlen's book *What Mothers Do* is great, and *Baby Talk* by Sally Ward offer lots of clear and fun suggestions for playing with your baby in ways that help them to thrive (see Further Reading).

Recognizing joint pressures and the different phases in a long and changing relationship can be important too. One mom commented to me: "Tiredness really is the enemy of intimacy—I'm sure that's what kills your sex drive as much as your hormones." Another says: "My husband and I have had to work hard at remembering we are still a married couple and not just Tom's parents." This may be true for you for a while, but it's also short-lived and, over the course of a long and happy relationship, it's just a period to be assimilated. It may help if your partner understands that too, as this new mom discovered:

> There have been difficult times when my husband and I have had blazing rows simply because we've both been so tired...but we've managed to talk everything through and I would say our relationship is stronger than ever now.
>
> *Tess, mother of a 6-month-old daughter*

Adapting alongside your partner can help you both to grow:

> Having babies brought my husband and me closer—you have a third party to discuss...I'm a lot less self-absorbed and I have learned a bit more patience!
>
> *Vicki, mother of 4- and 6-year-old daughters*

In addition, you'll find that some friendships change, often unexpectedly, which can mean couples lean more on each other, as another mom points out:

> I don't have as much time for some friends but more time for other ones so, I suppose dynamics have changed. The relationship with your partner moves up a level because you always have a bond that no one else has.
>
> *Louise, mother of a 1-year-old daughter*
> *and a 3-year-old son*

It is helpful at this time to have an appreciation of each other's different but equal roles, responsibilities, and contributions. And they really are different, but equal.

New parents need to be sensitive to what parenting truly involves and to the fact that there is no off-duty time with a newborn—this can extend right through the baby stage. However, if both partners are contributing fairly, they can give each other necessary breaks and support. As a new mom you will probably have six weeks of maternity leave, and some women take longer. New dads can choose to take some paternity leave—my advice is to arrange between you that this happens. Your baby's first days and weeks are a precious time that doesn't come back, plus you will need some help as you regain your strength. Once things settle down, it's important that the working parent's contribution is not seen as help—it is contributing to and taking part in a shared life. Now is not the time for dad to head off to the gym every night after work; it is the time for him to get home for the bedtime routine. Your children will benefit from their time with him, and you may be grateful for the break. Child care and household tasks need to be divided fairly (and *fair* doesn't mean half if one partner works outside the home, but neither does fair mean that mom is also cook, cleaner, housekeeper, financial manager, insurance broker, shopper, teacher, nurse, butler, laundry maid, and general grunt, all on four hours sleep!) A good tip for the working parent of a baby is, never ask an at-home partner "Can I help?", "What shall I do?", or "I'll do such-and-such," as well as each of you having mutually agreed areas of responsibility, might make for a happier and more equal relationship.

In *Plain Living*, Lucretia Mott wrote in 1850:

> In the true marriage relationship
> The independence of husband and wife is equal,
> Their dependence mutual.
> And their obligations reciprocal.

If you are married, how would you define a true marriage relationship?

I have a good spiritual director who said to me, "Go and enjoy that baby of yours!" It is good advice for both parents, and it is easier to do if, like everything else, it is shared.

As you think about these things with your partner, you might find this passage from 1 Corinthians 12:4–7 helpful to talk about. What does it mean for the two of you?

Now there are varieties of gifts, but the same Spirit; and there are varieties of service, but the same Lord; and there are varieties of activities, but it is the same God who activates all of them in everyone. To each is given the manifestation of the Spirit for the common good.

Try to hold onto the values that made your relationship work in the first place. I remember on one early date with my husband, soon after we had met, we each thought of the two things we wanted most from our ideal relationship. Mine at the time were passion and empathy, Stephen's were honesty and equality. It was a light moment, but we went on to talk about other things that we thought were important: faith, peace, loving kindness, freedom—every couple will have their own ideas. Every now and then, we do a quick check to make sure we still have those values at the center, despite life's many changes, because that's what works for us. One friend makes the point that it is important to keep investing in each other:

From when the children were quite small we have always had regular babysitters. We try to retain our "Love Night" each week, which is when we do something special, either at home or out somewhere—it's very easy to become wrapped up in a new baby and forget that your partner has their own needs.

Jane, mother of an 8-year-old daughter and a 5-year-old son

If you really are feeling at the end of your rope, take a minute to reflect on one of these ideas:

- "I've learned that people will forget what you said, people will forget what you did, but people will never forget how you made them feel" (Maya Angelou).

Your baby feels safe and loved with you, whatever mistakes you might feel you make from day to day. You are all your baby needs, just as you are.

• "Think of all the beauty still left around you and be happy'"(Anne Frank).

Look around you now, and find one beautiful thing. Enjoy it for its own sake for a few seconds.

• In the middle of all the changes you are experiencing, enjoy the wonder of your baby. In the words of this mother:

Being greeted with the most enormous grin and big wide open arms reaching up for a cuddle makes everything else just pale into insignificance!

Tracey, mother of an 8-month-old daughter

• Take a few moments to really look at the palm of your hand —the skin, the lines, the colors, and textures. Then, hold your baby's little hand and do the same. Think about the words below. What sort of impact do they have on you?

If you look deeply into the palm of your hand, you will see your parents and all generations of your ancestors. All of them are alive in this moment. Each is present in your body. You are the continuation of each of these people.

Thich Nhat Hanh

Wow! Part of the miracle of life is its fluidity and pace. It isn't static, but it is incredible.

Loving Our Colorful Children

Life is like a kaleidoscope—the shape, patterns, colors, and dynamics shift and change. Sometimes the changes are striking and they make us gasp; other times the changes are subtle. Either way, they are often unexpected and even if we know a change is coming, we won't be able to predict exactly how the shape, patterns, and colors will shift. It can be tempting, when faced with a change like a pregnancy or a new baby, to want to get life back to normal as soon as possible, without realizing that it will be a new normality. These events are like throwing all the jigsaw pieces of your life up into the air and seeing where they land, and which ones you will pick up first to start your new picture. If we can prepare ourselves for this, then it can be a beautiful experience—a turn of life's brilliant kaleidoscope.

However many parenting manuals we might read, nothing can prepare us for parenthood better than our own children. Getting to know and respect the child you've actually got, rather than an ideal baby in a book or in one's preconceived ideas, and being shaped in part by their real needs, real responses, and real personality, is important—and a privilege.

When I asked one mom about how she viewed her parenting role, she said:

> Your child is a whole different person than you with their own life force, not as you perhaps imagine while pregnant, a combination of you and your partner. For this reason, it's important to try and accept the child as they are and for who they are—try to accept their uniqueness...I'm not sure that your role is really to teach children too much, more to keep them safe and give them a firm emotional foundation so they can develop the best they can, for they will grow up with or without you, you just want it to be optimally. I'd be delighted if my children turned out to be warm and loving and quite sensible, and even a bit more grown up than myself.
>
> *Hannah, mother of an 8-month-old daughter and*
> *a 2½-year-old daughter*

This mother adds:

> I knew I would love them, but I have truly delighted in finding I like them as people.

- If you could write your own job description for parenthood, what would it be?

- If you could compare your version with other people's, how far would this be challenging and how far would it be affirming? What might you learn in each case?

When I thought about the best relationship I wanted to have with my children, I hit on three things: I'd like to *love, understand,* and *enjoy* my children, and I'd like them to feel and know that is what I'm doing because I hope that will help them to be happy and secure.

Another mom I know says that the most important things she wants to pass on to her children are:

A sense of security, happiness, and being loved.

Rachel, 16 weeks pregnant and
mother of five sons aged between 1 and 8

And then this mom says:

I want him to grow up knowing he is not only completely and utterly loved by my husband and I (and the rest of the family), but also by God and that nothing will ever change that.

Jenna, 7 months pregnant and mother of a 2-year-old son

I have found the following thoughts helpful. What thoughts and feelings do the following reflections inspire in you?

- Our children are given to us for a time to cherish, to protect, to nurture, and then to salute as they go their separate ways. They too have the light of God within, and a family should be a learning community in which children not only learn skills and values from parents, but in which adults learn new ways of experiencing things and seeing things through young eyes. From their birth on, let us cultivate the habit of dialogue and receptive listening. We should respect their right to grow into wholeness, not just the wholeness we may wish for them. If we lead fulfilling lives ourselves, we can avoid overprotecting them or trying to live through them.

Elizabeth Watson

- Small babies...need comfort, warmth and cherishing, yet they can equally kick and scream to demonstrate their independent will. From the cradle to maturity the desire to belong and, at the same time, the need to assert our independent existence, are in constant tension...A child that feels it is understood and loved will find it easier to develop inner security...Do we try to understand the difficulties, stresses and failures of our growing children and make them fully aware that, come what may, they are loved? This does not mean that we give them unlimited license. They still need an adequate framework within which it is safe to experiment and rebel.

  Rosalind Priestman

- I think parents need to be aware of how vital it is to leave everything to answer a young child's reaching out to you to "come quickly" to share a sunset or the beauty of a discovered wild flower, or the trick of the pet dog, or to listen with full attention, no matter what seems prior on your agenda, when children burst into the house from school eager to have you listen to a tale of woe or a triumph they have experienced during the day. There is little question that if as a parent we have not taken the time to really listen to children when they are young, listened not only to their words but to their feelings behind the words, they are unlikely to want to come with their sharings in later life. Learning to listen to each other in families can help us to make better listeners to others and to the Inner Guide.

  Dorothy Steere

Being a Parent

We have looked at how having a baby might challenge and change our images of God. It can also challenge and change our images of parenthood—images often formed in our own childhood and also by the media and well-meaning friends. It may be helpful to take a few moments to think about your own views and assumptions about what a parent is. There is a scene in Charles Dickens' *Dombey and Son* where the father who has neglected his daughter in favor of his son meets the young girl:

"Come here, Florence," said her father, coldly. "Do you know who I am?"

"Yes, Papa."

He is stern and remote, and she is meek and subdued, yet by the end of the story, when his daughter has grown up, he must swallow his pride, own his past mistakes, and accept her kindness if he is to live out the rest of his days happily.

Of course, we don't live in a Victorian melodrama, but stereotypes such as this can give us some helpful labels to think about in terms of our own parenting styles. Just as with our images of God, stereotypes of a mother and a father do often exist in our subconscious, so it's worth looking at which ones are helpful and which are not. Consider, for instance, the concept of a parent as a creator and guardian, compared to that of owner, investor, or director. Friend, caregiver, teacher, and police officer and judge might be other images to think about. How about probation officer and adviser-guide? How far are these concepts and stereotypes associated with one gender or another for you? How far might we aspire to one model but inadvertently slip into another from time to time? What value and connotations do we attach to each of these models? What do these terms mean to you? What effect might each model have on a child, and which most closely matches the type of parent you would like to be? How is this going to be expressed in your family life?

As we saw in chapter 4 of this book, the images we have of our parents and the images we have of God are often linked, so it can be helpful to look at both our images of God and our images of what makes a good or bad parent as we reflect on our own preferred style of parenting. For instance, I'm sure no one sets out to police their children, but sometimes we can end up doing that if we haven't thought in advance about how we will respond to certain situations. We might aspire to be an adviser-guide, but what does that mean at 4 AM when everyone is tired and kids of any age are acting up? It is important to be aware, most of the time, of our intentions and motivations so that we are at least acting on our reflections and not by accident. Part of those reflections might well include the thought that we cannot control the outcome—children are created by artists, not designed by architects.

Anne Frank wrote: "Parents can only give good advice or put them on the right paths, but the final forming of a person's character lies in their own hands." Anne was young when she recorded her thoughts, but wise and imaginative. The Jewish commandment to "Honor your father and your mother" has arguably led to much angst in the therapist's room from people who feel, for whatever reason, that they cannot, and also to a style of parenting in which parents are seen as overly strict and authoritative, beyond questioning. However, there are other ways of helpfully seeing this commandment as an underscoring of the importance of honor and respect within family relationships. If you want your children to respect you, to be proud of you and of their connection with you, what are the implications of this desire for the way you will behave toward your children? What do you need to do, what manner do you need to develop, in order that you might have this sort of relationship with your children? It is not your right to be honored by your children, but what are your responsibilities if you want them to honor you? Rabbi Abraham Joshua Heschel writes:

I am a father, I have a daughter. I love her dearly. And I would like her to obey the commandments of the Torah. I would like her to revere me as her father. And I asked myself the question again and again, "what is there about me that would be worth her reverence?" Unless I live a life that would deserve her reverence, I would make it impossible for her to live a life of Judaism.

Kenneth Barnes writes:

We cannot hope to transfer more than a little of our wisdom to our young people...We have increasingly to stand back...

This is the moment of disengagement, when parents must tell themselves that the young people are no longer their children and that they are outside their discipline...They cannot live their children's lives for them.

It is also the moment for parents to tell themselves that their children are not alone. They are in the hands of God. God does not offer any kind of perfection in the actual circumstances of life, nor freedom from exposure to evil. Nor will parents ever be able—if they are honest—to look back over their experience of parenthood without being conscious of imperfections in their own understanding and handling of their children.

What is your response to these thoughts?

Interpersonal Circles: Myself and My Changing Relationship Dynamics

Who we are, as individuals and in relationship to others, has an impact on our strengths, hopes, and achievements. Our sense of identity rests in part on the balance between who we are as unique individuals and who we are in relation to other people. Watch the popular and award-winning film *Amelie* and notice how in the first ten minutes (after the credits) people are described and defined both as individuals and in relationship with each other. This is all challenged with the arrival of a baby. Having a baby brings natural but noticeable changes, including the new role of parent if this is your first child, and a new relationship to add to your life and to nurture. The following reflective activity may help you to explore this as the new roles and relationships within your family start to develop.

You'll need a plain piece of paper. If you could draw a circle on this paper to represent yourself, what would it be like? Think about what size you want your circle to be, what color it will be, what pattern it might be filled in with, and where on the paper you want to draw it. Draw that circle, then do exactly the same for each member of your family and each of your closest friends. Where will their circles go in relation to your own? What size will they be, and what color? If you are pregnant, you may want to include your baby. Next, add more distant relatives, other friends, acquaintances. Think about each area of life and fill in as many circles as possible, making a map of everyone you know, trying to include all your relationships. Use symbolic colors rather than names, and think about where each one will go in relation to yourself (see the circles diagram on page 125).

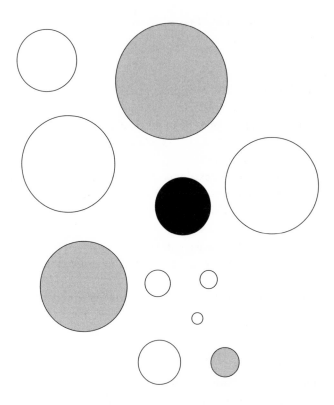

As you draw, keep in mind:

- Where will you put each circle in relation to you?
- What size will each circle be, and what color? They can all be different.
- How will you decide to show who is most important, who is closest to you?
- Do you want to include your baby?
- You may like to include people who are no longer alive, and also pets.
- You might like to include a circle for God. Where will God be on your paper?

Now analyze your circles. Take a close look at your finished circles. What might they tell you about:

- Yourself?
- Your children and/or your pregnancy "bump"?
- Who you are closest to?
- People you might like to be more close to?
- People you might like to be less close to?
- Your family dynamics?
- Your priorities, agendas, concerns, and desires?
- People who dominate, and people who hold back?
- Anything you would like to change, or anything that is changing anyway?
- What you hope the pattern on your paper might be in a month, a year, two years, and what steps you could take to influence this development?
- Whether this activity has raised anything you'd like to pray about?

Human Connection

Human beings are fundamentally all the same. We are made of human flesh, human bones and blood. What is more, our internal feelings—desires, hopes and ambitions—are the same: we all want to avoid suffering and achieve happiness. And we all have an equal right to be happy. In other words, we are all part of one big human family, which includes all of humankind on this planet.

His Holiness the Dalai Lama

In the well-known extract from one of his sermons (see the box on p. 127), John Donne explores the idea that individuals are all connected to each other through death. Can the same be said of birth? If you want to, try substituting the dying words with birth words in this extract, as I have done. I found this a delicate thing to do, so please do tweak it, as my version won't be to everyone's liking, but it is about life, however you make sense of it.

When one man dies *[is born]*, one chapter is not torn out of *[is added to]* the book, but translated into a better language, and every chapter must be so translated.

God employs several translators; some pieces are translated by age *[birth]*, some by sickness *[IVF]*, some by war *[cesarean]*, some by justice *[adoption]*, but *God's hand is in every translation*, and his hand shall bind up all our scattered leaves again for that library where every book shall lie open to one another...

No man is an island, entire of itself; every man is a piece of the continent, a part of the main.

Explore your responses to some of the ideas in the extract, and in the words of the Dalai Lama quoted above, in the light of your experiences of pregnancy and motherhood:

- Although we are all individuals, we are all connected to each other, so whatever happens to one person affects other people. Does it?
- "Human beings are fundamentally all the same." Are we?
- Focus on the line of John Donne's sermon which says "No man is an island." Compare this with part of the Dalai Lama's words at the beginning of this section: "We [all] belong to one big human family, which includes all of humankind on this planet." And also with a quote from the Islamic Hadith: "If any single part of the body aches, the whole body feels the effects and rushes to its relief." What are your thoughts and feelings about these ideas in terms of your own family relationships?
- Try the following exercise once while pregnant and then after the birth of your baby, and again on your baby's first birthday. If your children are older, try it now and then again in six months. Expect some changes as you adapt to your changing family life and as your family grows, and honor them:

This is what I

think...
feel...
value...
need...
aspire to...
want...
love...
hate...
fear...
desire...
believe...
am committed to...

You are the bows from which your children as living arrows are sent forth...Let your bending in the archer's hand be for gladness; for even as He loves the arrow that flies, so He loves also the bow that is stable.

Kahlil Gibran, artist and writer, in The Prophet

Conclusion

You can be sure that when you have a baby, you will change and your relationships will change. This can be both difficult and wonderful. If you look after your inner reserves and keep communicating with your loved ones, your inner self, and with God, then you will find that all this is leading to a great treasure. Having a baby can open up depths of love you never knew you had—all these changes can be transforming. In the words of Anne Frank:

> Everyone has inside… a piece of good news. The good news is that you don't know how great you can be! How much you can love! What you can accomplish! And what your potential is!

I hope you embrace your journey as you discover life's potential for joy, together with your wonderful new baby.

Endnotes

Chapter 1

1. Rufus M. Jones, Quaker, 1948.
2. George Fox, in *Quaker Faith and Practice*.
3. Siegen-Smith, Nikki. *Welcome to the World: A Celebration of Birth and Babies from Many Cultures*. (New York: Orchard Books, 1996.)
4. *Quaker Faith and Practice*.
5. Aron, Elaine. *The Highly Sensitive Child: Helping Our Children Thrive When the World Overwhelms Them*. (New York: HarperCollins, 2003.)
6. Merryweather, Sr. Sheila Julian. *Colourful Prayer: A New Way to Pray When Words Are Inadequate*. (Suffolk, England: Kevin Mayhew, 2004.)
7. This drawing by an anonymous nine-year-old appears *in My Shalom, My Peace: Paintings and Drawing of Jewish and Arab Children*. Edited by Jacob Zim and Ofek Uriel. Translated by Dov Vardi. (New York: McGraw-Hill, 1975.)

Chapter 2

1. Markova, Dawna. "Living Wide Open: Landscapes of the Mind," in *I Will Not Die an Unlived Life*. (Newburyport, MA: Conari Press, 2000.) See Dr. Markova's Web site at www.smartwired.org.
2. Hanh, Thich Nhat. *Peace Is Every Step: The Path of Mindfulness in Everyday Life*. (New York: Bantam [reissue edition], 1992.)
3. Silf, Margaret. *Sacred Spaces: Stations on a Celtic Way*. (Orleans, MA: Paraclete Press, 2001.)
4. Bella Brown, in *Quaker Faith and Practice*.

Chapter 4

1. Williamson, Marianne. "Our Deepest Fear" from *A Return To Love: Reflections on the Principles of A Course in Miracles.* (New York: Harper Collins, 1992, pp. 190–191.)
2. George Fox, in *Quaker Faith and Practice.*
3. Estés, Clarissa Pinkola. *Women Who Run With the Wolves: Myths and Stories of the Wild Woman Archetype.* (New York: Ballantine Books, 1996.)
4. Silf, Margaret. *Inner Compass: An Introduction to Ignatian Spirituality.* (Chicago: Loyola Press, 1999.)

Further Reading

Adam, David. *Landscapes of Light: An Illustrated Anthology of Prayers.* London: Society for Promoting Christian Knowledge, 2001.

Aron, Elaine. *The Highly Sensitive Child: Helping Our Children Thrive When the World Overwhelms Them.* New York: HarperCollins, 2003.

Ashwin, Angela. *Patterns Not Padlocks: For Parents and All Busy People.* Guildford, UK: Eagle Publishing, 2002.

Delaney, Sue. 2005. "Women Beginning a Spiritual Quest," *The Way: A Review of Christian Spirituality,* 44 (1):33–44.

Estés, Clarissa Pinkola. *Women Who Run With the Wolves: Myths and Stories of the Wild Woman Archetype.* New York: Ballantine Books, 1996.

Frank, Anne. *The Diary of a Young Girl.* New York: Puffin, 2002.

Giles, Gordon. *The Harmony of Heaven: Musical Meditations for Lent and Easter.* Oxford, UK: Bible Reading Fellowship, 2003.

Guenther, Margaret. *Holy Listening: The Art of Spiritual Direction.* London: Darton, Longman & Todd, 1992.

Hebblethwaite, Margaret. *Motherhood and God.* London: Geoffrey Chapman, 1993.

Heschel, Abraham Joshua and Heschel, Susannah. *Moral Grandeur and Spiritual Audacity: Essays.* New York: Farrar Straus Giroux, 1997.

Hill, Melissa. *The Smart Woman's Guide Staying at Home.* London: Vermilion, 2001.

Jackson, Deborah. *Three in a Bed: The Benefits of Sleeping With Your Baby.* London: Bloomsbury Publishing, 2003.

Jackson, Deborah. *When Your Baby Cries.* London: Hodden & Stroughton, 2004.

Liedloff, Jean. *The Continuum Concept: In Search of Happiness Lost.* New York: Penguin, 1986.

Linn, Dennis, Linn Sheila Fabricant, and Linn, Matthew. *Good Goats: Healing Our Image of God*. Mahwah, NJ: Paulist Press, 1994.

McKay, Pinky. *Parenting by Heart*. Lothian Books, 2003. (Also see her Web site at <http.//www.pinky-mychild.com>)

Merryweather, Sister Sheila Julian. *Colourful Prayer: A New Way to Pray When Words Are Inadequate*. Suffolk, UK: Kevin Mayhew, 2004.

Nhat Hanh, Thich. *Peace Is Every Step: The Path of Mindfulness in Everyday Life*. London: Rider, 1995.

Pantley, Elizabeth. *The No-Cry Sleep Solution: Gentle Ways to Help Your Baby Sleep Through the Night*. New York: McGraw-Hill, 2002.

Quaker Faith and Practice. Quaker Books, 2005.

Sears, William and Sears, Martha. *The Fussy Baby Book: Parenting Your High-Need Child From Birth to Five*. London: Harper Thorsons, 2005.

Shuttle, Penelope. *The Orchard Upstairs*. Oxford, UK: Oxford University Press, 1980.

Siegen-Smith, Nikki. *Welcome to the World: A Celebration of Birth and Babies From Many Cultures*. Bath, UK: Barefoot Books, 2005.

Silf, Margaret. *Inner Compass: An Introduction to Ignatian Spirituality*. Chicago: Loyola Press, 1999.

Silf, Margaret. *Sacred Spaces: Stations on a Celtic Way*. Oxford, UK: Lion Hudson, 2005.

Slee, Nicola. *The Book of Mary*. London: Society for Promoting Christian Knowledge, 2007.

Stadlen, Naomi. *What Mothers Do, Especially When It Looks Like Nothing*. London: Piatkus Books, 2004.

Ward, Sally. *Baby Talk*. Arrow Books, 2004.

Whitmire, Catherine. *Plain Living: A Quaker Path to Simplicity*. Notre Dame, IN: Sorin Books, 2001.

Wicks, Robert J. *Everyday Simplicty: A Practice Guide to Spiritual Growth*. Notre Dame, IN: Sorin Books, 2000.

Wolf, Naomi. *Misconceptions: Truth, Lies and the Unexpected on the Journey to Motherhood*. London: Vintage, 2002.

Zim, Jacob (ed). *My Shalom, My Peace: Paintings and Poems by Jewish and Arab Children*. New York: McGraw-Hill, 1975.